Getting Involved!

A Guide to Hunting and Conservation

For Kids!

Wildlife Area →

Getting Involved!

A Guide to Hunting
and
Conservation

For Kids!

by

Sue Watkins

Illustrations by Emily J. Biggs

Design by Diana Schultz

SAFARI PRESS

GETTING INVOLVED! A Guide to Hunting and Conservation for Kids © 2011 by Sue Watkins. Illustrations © 2011 by Emily J. Biggs and design © 2011 by Diana Schultz. No part of this publication may be used or reproduced in any form or by any means without permission from the publisher.

The trademark Safari Press ® is registered with the U.S. Patent and Trademark Office and in other countries.

Watkins, Sue

First edition

Safari Press

2010 Long Beach, California

ISBN 978-1-57157-377-3

Library of Congress Catalog Card Number: 2010924113

10 9 8 7 6 5 4 3 2 1

Printed in China

Readers wishing to receive the Safari Press catalog, featuring many fine books on big-game hunting, wingshooting, and sporting firearms, should write to Safari Press Inc., P.O. Box 3095, Long Beach, CA 90803, USA. Tel: (714) 894-9080 or visit our Web site at www.safaripress.com.

Table of Contents

A Note to Parents and Teachers

This book has been many years in the making, not on paper, but in my head. I spent twelve very influential years of my life working at a wildlife park and then at a zoo as an animal trainer and educational lecturer. I visited thousands of children through the school assembly program, teaching wildlife conservation and education. I was an antihunter, convinced that a love of animals and concern for the environment were enough to save our wildlife. At that time my experience led me to believe that humans just needed to stay out of the natural world in order for wildlife to flourish.

Twenty years later I was still holding on to my antihunting beliefs when I met a big-game hunter. I was intrigued to discover what would make someone want to kill our wildlife. I felt certain that hunters could not possibly have the same love for wildlife that dominated my own life. And so my journey began.

I immersed myself into the world of both the hunter and the hunted. What I discovered shocked me. Hunters and fishermen pay for more wildlife conservation in the United States today than all other members of society combined! I didn't want to believe it, but the facts were staring me right in the face. I had to let go of my well-intentioned yet naïve antihunting views, for I realized they were doing more harm than good.

This book teaches children the truth about hunting and the role it plays in the conservation of our wildlife. It gives children ways to get involved in conservation projects, hunting programs, and shooting sports. It in no way encourages them to become little Rambos, but instead leads them into our natural world by encouraging thoughtful, ethical, and responsible sportsmanship for both boys and girls. I would encourage you as the adult, parent, or teacher to read it first. The message is clear.

The future of our wildlife will rely heavily on the hunter of tomorrow.

Acknowledgments

I wish to thank the following organizations for contributing information and photographs that made this book possible: California Waterfowl Association, the National Wild Turkey Federation, National 4-H Headquarters, U.S. Department of Agriculture, Pheasants Forever, Quail Forever, Safari Club International, the National Rifle Association, California Department of Fish and Game, Kalkomey Enterprises, Inc, Conservation Force, the United States Fish and Wildlife Service, and the Kansas State Historical Museum.

I need to acknowledge Bill Adams and Jim Russell for their knowledge and contributions in the overall areas of hunting, safety, and ethics. A special thanks to Keegan Hammond, Kerissa Nelson, Justine McQueary, Ashley Bishop, and Jon Michael McGrath II for sharing their inspirational stories with today's youth. I also wish to acknowledge the following people for providing photographs: page x–xi by James Leash; page 17 (male and female wood ducks) by Diana Schultz; page 16 (two wood ducks peeking out of box) by Jim Schlotter; pages 15–16 (hatchlings jumping) and (male and female wood ducks on box) by Don Lange; page 39 by Harry Bunfill; and page 56 by Craig Hancock.

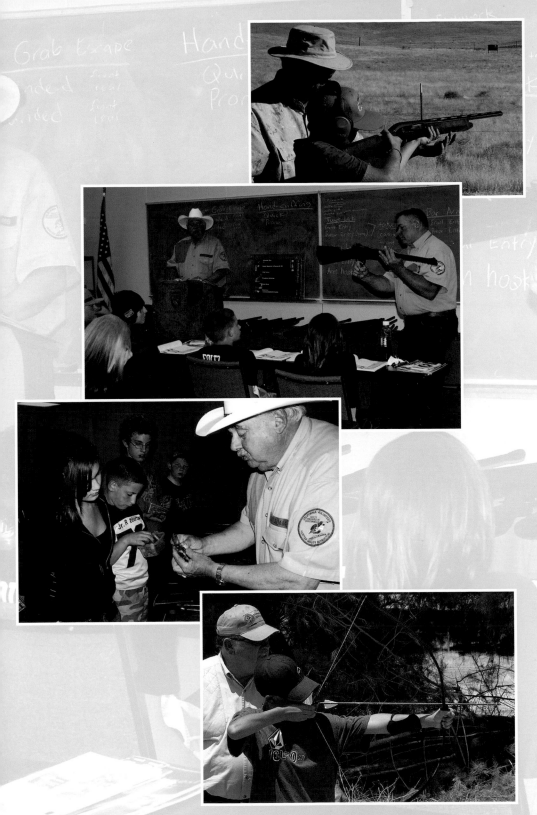

Tell me, and I forget
Show me, and I remember
Involve me, and I understand

I'm only going to ask you to do this once in this book, and it is now.

Re-read those top three lines.... OK, that is what I want you to do.

A Guide to Getting Involved in Hunting and Conservation is divided into four parts. The first part tells you about the relationship between hunting and conservation, how it went wrong in the past, and why it is important today. The second part of the book shows you how various organizations involve kids in hunting or wildlife conservation projects, such as overnight camps, wood duck projects, and even art. It also shows you what these organizations have done to ensure the survival of various species. The third part of the book looks at the modern-day hunter. He or she is not the old yahoo of years past! Today's hunter is an ethical person dedicated to conservation. We'll look at what's involved in hunter education courses, and we'll discover the cool jobs that state and federal wildlife agents have. They are like the CSI of wildlife! Last, we want to involve you, so there is a state-by-state section that shows you how to get involved no matter where you live.

I hope this book opens your eyes to the importance of hunting and why it is needed to ensure the survival of many animals. But most of all, I want you to Get Involved.

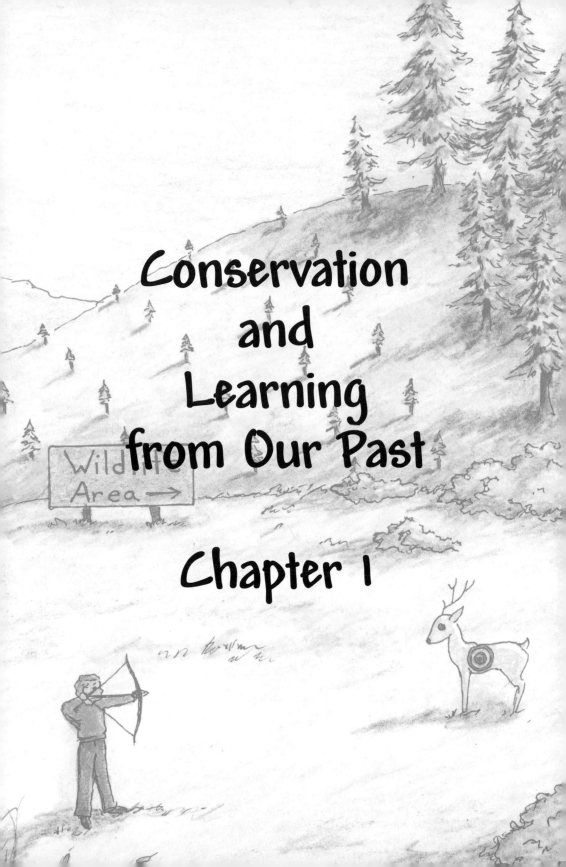

Conservation and Learning from Our Past

Chapter 1

What's This All About?

Conservation has become a very important action in the world today. Most likely, you see something every day that deals with conservation. At the bookstore, you may see books printed on recycled paper, and on the streets you may see cars that are hybrids. They run on gasoline and electric power. Cities often use buses that are natural gas/clean air vehicles. Your neighborhood may even have extra trash cans, one for recyclables only. Even if you don't know it, you conserve every day, perhaps with a little help from your parents. By turning off the

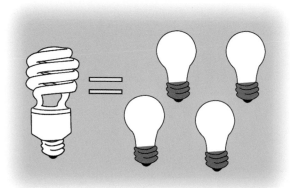

lights as you leave the room, you're conserving, or saving power. If you ride a bike or walk to school, you're conserving gas.

Products that are labeled "green" are most likely produced from recycled goods or are a more environmentally friendly replacement for something, such as fluorescent light bulbs for incandescent bulbs. We think it's pretty cool that just by switching from a regular light bulb to a compact fluorescent you'll be using four times less energy! (Fluorescent bulbs also last much longer.)

Conservation

That's a pretty familiar word. If we look in the dictionary, we would find the following definition: con·ser·va·tion: 1. A careful preservation and protection of something, planned management of a natural resource to prevent exploitation, destruction, or neglect.

Conservation involves not only the management of resources, like electricity, water, and gas, through more efficient use, but it also involves the planned management of both habitat and animals. To thrive, animals need vast undisturbed areas of land. These areas must afford a proper habitat

Joe cannot sell his cars on protected land. He can't spell, either.

for the animals and supply both water and food. Today's modern-day hunter provides these through land purchases, easements, habitat enhancement, and funding. These conservation actions ensure the survival of many species.

Are you still reading? We lose some kids on that last paragraph! You're probably thinking, "This is a line of baloney; hunters don't protect wildlife, they kill it! That is perhaps what you believe, or what you've been told. But what people do (their actions) or don't do (their nonactions), always tells us the truth.

There is a saying: "Actions speak louder than words." It means that most people react more to what you do than what you say. We're going to show you what hunters do, how they help the environment, and how you can get involved. Who knows, maybe you, too, will become not only a conservationist but a hunter as well.

Easements

Easements are like permission slips you get in school. They give permission for someone to use another person's land for a particular use. A wildlife or conservation easement may allow others to improve the land for wildlife and for hunting, but would not allow them to, let's say, sell automobiles there. It only allows for certain things.

Doing the Right Thing

Most people try to do the right thing, but we've all done the wrong thing once or twice as well. In fact, sometimes we learn faster by doing the wrong thing first. Have you ever touched a hot burner and got a nasty burn? Sure, we understood our parents when they said it was hot, but we learned it was hot a lot faster when we got burned. Throwing footballs in the house is the same idea. Until we break something, it all just seems to be OK. For mankind, learning about some aspects of the earth and nature has been like burning your finger. We didn't learn our lesson until it was too late, and by that time we'd already been burned.

A Dirty Past

Look around your house, down your street, and around your neighborhood. Chances are, they look pretty clean. That's because we've cleaned up our act. Conservation (the managing of our resources) has greatly improved over the years. Mankind currently has a pretty clean slate, and our future is bright (as you will see in the next chapters), but we do have a dirty past!

Ever wonder what happens when you flush a toilet? Where does all the waste from millions of people go? Well, today, cities have complex

Wow!

Hunters and fishermen pay more for wildlife conservation than all others in society combined!
*Conservation Force

sewer systems that treat raw sewage with a variety of chemicals that make it safe for it to be released back into the environment. But it was not always that way. Back in the 1700s, many communities had open trenches stretching

along the streets and from house to house. This is where people dumped their raw sewage.

But it didn't stay there. The trenches with all the raw sewage flowed like a stream into the nearest lake or river, turning a once clear body of water into a large toilet bowl. To make matters worse, people then used this same water to wash their clothes in and to drink from! People back then thought that the sewage would dissolve in the water, but diseases caused by bacteria, viruses, and pathogens thrive in raw sewage. The water mixed with the sewage became deadly for people who wanted to drink it, bathe in it, or wash their clothes in it. So, as people drank the water, many got sick and many more died.

Not only did people die, but lakes and rivers also became "dead zones" because the fish and aquatic life died. It took years before some of the lakes and rivers recovered. This example shows how people in society have learned from the past.

We've learned a lot about hunting from our past mistakes as well. Today's hunters are a group of individuals who take pride in conserving wildlife and in preserving a healthy outdoors. But the same cannot be said about hunters of the past. This is one of the reasons why hunting received a bad name.

Pathogens

Infectious agents, commonly known as germs!

Bye-Bye Buffalo

As ambassadors of the United States, these big hairy beasts once roamed from Canada to Mexico and our best estimates say there were about sixty million of them!

Photo courtesy of Kansas State Historical Society.

There were so many of them roaming across the plains that early explorers described their experiences in encountering them as "the plains black, and appeared as if in motion." There were buffalo as far as the eye could see. So what happened to them?

Unregulated hunting nearly killed off the American buffalo. As early as the 1600s demand for buffalo fur started in Europe. Then at the beginning of the 1800s, buffalo hides and buffalo tongues became more popular, and over the next eighty years, buffalo were killed at an astonishing rate. In Montana alone, just one merchant sold 250,000 hides during the 1881–1882 season.

A man sits on a stack of 250,000 buffalo hides in 1874. (Photo courtesy of Kansas State Historical Society)

Individual hunters seeking profit were not the only problem. Market hunters did the most damage. These people killed animals in huge quantities to sell the meat and hides to restaurants, stores, and individuals. Train companies offered tourists the opportunity to shoot as many buffalo as possible, right out of the window! These tourists would only stop shooting if they ran out of ammunition or if their guns got too hot! There were even buffalo killing contests! One shooter in Kansas killed 120 buffalo in forty minutes!

The most famous buffalo killer, was "Buffalo" Bill Cody, a Wyoming native known for his "entertaining personality." Bill Cody shot and killed more than four thousand animals in just two years! This was not hunting, it was slaughter! By 1883, hunters began coming home empty-handed because they simply could not find any buffalo left to shoot. Hunters had killed almost all of the buffalo in North America!

Luckily a few remained, well hidden from hunters. By 1893, after long searches for wild buffalo, only a few hundred remained in the newly formed Yellowstone National Park in Montana. With their population going from 60 million to a couple hundred, buffalo were in danger of

"Buffalo" Bill Cody.

extinction. Concerned about their survival, the American Bison Society was formed in 1905 by William Hornaday, a zoologist and a hunter, and President Theodore Roosevelt, a hunter. Together they established a number of wildlife preserves and private ranches so that the few remaining buffalo could seek protection. Slowly their numbers grew, and today the National Buffalo Association estimates that there are 150,000 buffalo roaming the United States.

In order to manage the herds, regulated hunting of buffalo is allowed. But today's hunters, unlike the buffalo hunters of the past, participate in the hunting of buffalo not only for sport, but in order to pay for their management and save the species. About 90 percent of buffalo today live on land owned by private individuals, and the owners of these buffalo "sell" buffalo hunts in order to pay for their care. It may cost the hunter anywhere from $1,600 to $5,000 to shoot one bull buffalo. The number of buffalo shot each year is carefully monitored so that the herds continue to grow.

At this point you may be wondering, why shoot them at all? Why not just let them live? The answer lies in why hunters are so important to conservation. Remember, 90 percent of today's buffalo live on privately owned land. The people who own the land and manage the herds need to make a living; somehow, the land has to pay for itself. If we didn't have people willing to pay to shoot a buffalo, most likely the owners of the buffalo would sell off their land to developers (to build houses) or would use the land to farm. Instead, they have a choice, and they choose to leave the land wild. Uninhabited, or wild, land supports healthy herds of buffalo and provides many acres of habitat for other wild animals as well. Thus, the people who sell buffalo hunts are, indeed, making a huge contribution to the survival of the species. Without them and without the hunters, the buffalo would be confined to our national parks, which can only support small populations.

Today's hunter is nothing like the market or sport hunter of the past. Currently, there are 147 million people in the United States who either hunt or fish. The U.S. Fish & Wildlife Service reported that in the year 2003 alone, hunters and fishermen spent over 600 million dollars on just hunting fees. All this money went toward the conservation of our wildlife. Today's modern hunters, not environmentalists, are the people who provide land, food, water, and shelter to our wildlife. Animals need this money to thrive!

So what makes a good, modern-day hunter? Today's hunters come from all walks of life. They may be lawyers, teachers, corporate bankers, or factory workers. They may be retired or working, own their own ranches, or hunt on public land. They are old and young, and many of today's hunters are kids! These kids aren't hanging at the mall or sitting indoors watching T.V. They're out riding on ATVs (all terrain vehicles), fishing from boats, making wood duck boxes, and hunting! The next chapter will show you what they do!

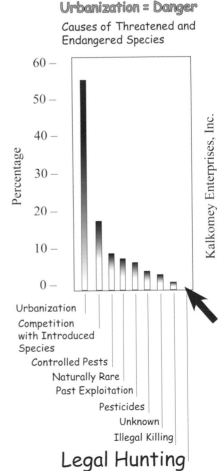

Urbanization = Danger

Causes of Threatened and Endangered Species

Kalkomey Enterprises, Inc.

Urbanization
Competition with Introduced Species
Controlled Pests
Naturally Rare
Past Exploitation
Pesticides
Unknown
Illegal Killing

Legal Hunting

Hunting & Shooting Organizations for Kids

Chapter 2

CALIFORNIA
WATERFOWL

Waterfowl Organizations

Duck Hunting

Duck hunting is extremely popular in many areas of the United States. It is often the first hunt for many kids. Hunters love their ducks, and there are many hunter-supported waterfowl organizations throughout the United States that have activities for youth. We're going to look at just one organization, but check the back of the book for an organization in your area.

California Waterfowl Is Not Just for Ducks!

It's for everyone, including kids! Like other waterfowl associations throughout the United States, California Waterfowl's main goal is to make sure that waterfowl (for example, ducks, geese, and swans) have enough protected land to thrive.

But waterfowl need the right kind of land—shopping malls and parking lots need not apply! People once believed that adding more wetlands (water) would increase duck populations, but they found that even with more water, duck populations did not grow. So California Waterfowl started protecting, restoring, and enhancing land throughout California. The organization plants trees, manages water flow, and provides food and habitat throughout the state by working with private individuals, other wildlife groups, and the state of California.

A Bad Choice Can Become a Better One!

An open field planted with green crops may look like a haven for a duck to make a nest, but it's a very bad choice because sooner or later the farmer will need to plow that field. California Waterfowl noticed that a lot of duck nests, eggs, and young hatchlings were accidentally run over by farmers. So the organization began to work closely with farmers, encouraging them to plant tall grasses and provide water along the edges of their fields that would be more attractive as nesting spots for ducks.

California Waterfowl also became involved with egg salvage, encouraging farmers to save nests found in their fields. Now, if a farmer spots a nest in the area he wants to plow, he can contact an egg-salvage facility. The facility will pick up the eggs and deliver them to a special incubator. The eggs are carefully watched until they hatch and then they are cared for until the ducklings are old enough to be released safely in the wild.

320,000
That's the number of acres California Waterfowl has enhanced, restored, or protected for ducks, geese, and swans!

The California Waterfowl Wood Duck Project

Wood ducks are found throughout the United States. They are colorful ducks that nest in tree cavities (holes in the tree). The female wood duck, or hen, will lay her eggs in this hole and sit on the eggs for about a month. Once the eggs hatch, the mother calls the chicks, and one by one they jump out of the tree to the ground. Wood duck ducklings have been known to jump fifty feet to the ground!

Because of habitat loss, many wood ducks rely on manmade boxes instead of trees to raise their young. Since 1991, California Waterfowl has been making boxes for wood ducks with the help of many volunteers. Over 500,000 wood ducks have hatched inside manmade California Waterfowl wood duck boxes!

The colorful male wood duck stands guard as the female flies into a manmade box to sit on the eggs.

It's a big world out there. With the hen calling, these hatchlings check out their next move.

And away they go!

Imagine jumping 50 feet at just one day old! These little guys are so light they float down and softly bounce on the ground.

You can build it yourself

California Waterfowl can provide you with instructions and plans on how to build your own wood duck box. The organization also has projects that show you how to monitor them (see who's using them) and record your success. Go to www.calwaterfowl.org Checking on the wood boxes is half the fun. Sometimes it is not eggs that you'll find, but squirrels, opossums, or other critters that think it's a good home for them, too.

The male (top) and female (bottom) wood ducks look quite different.

California Waterfowl's
Camp for Kids!

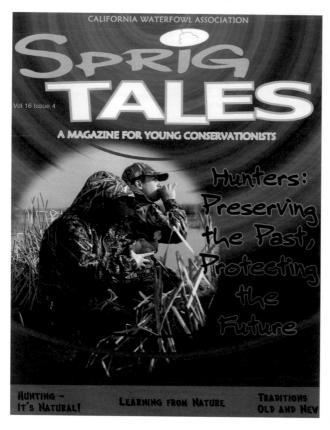

Perhaps you've never been to camp because you don't want to collect pine cones and sing camp songs. . . . Well, you won't be doing any of that in these camps! Youth hunter camps offer awesome activities and skills that every young hunter will enjoy.

There are many organizations like California Waterfowl all over the country. To see what hunter youth camps are in your area, check the organizations listed in the state-by-state listing in the back of this book. You may want to search the Internet for "youth waterfowl programs," and make sure to include your state. Hint: Many organizations offer partial scholarships to cover the cost of the camp. Search the site. You may qualify!

Check out www.calwaterfowl.org. You can also become a California Waterfowl Junior Sprig Member. You'll receive *Sprig Tales,* a magazine for young conservationists that is full of information and activities for young hunters.

Shooting clay pigeons is challenging.

Learning to call ducks is great fun!

In addition to getting your Hunter-Education Certificate, you can get expert instruction at the shotgun or rifle range.

Painting a decoy is a new experience for many campers.

Learning what gear you need when hunting—even if it doesn't fit so well—is part of the program!

Archery isn't as easy as it looks, but you'll get plenty of help. Keeping your arm straight and pulling back toward your ear is key!

Duck Stamps

Do I Need a Stamp to Go Duck Hunting?

That's right, stamps aren't just for postage! If you want to hunt ducks and you are sixteen or older, you need a duck stamp! In 1934 Congress passed the Duck Stamp Act. In order to hunt, you must buy a duck stamp and place it on your state hunting license. By buying a stamp, we raise money for land conservation.

When the program started, duck stamps cost $1.00 each. Today they cost $15.00 each. Since 1934, more than $600 million have been raised by hunters and others (such as stamp collectors) buying these stamps. All the money has been used to preserve and protect five million acres of wetland habitat for ducks.

But there's something even cooler about the duck stamp program. It's the Junior Duck Stamp Contest! Kids from all across the nation draw ducks, geese, and swans in an effort to raise money to conserve wildlife areas. This stamp is not used for hunting or postage, but it is sold at post offices throughout the United States as a way for kids to contribute to conservation projects.

About 24,500 of these stamps are sold each year, and each stamp costs $5.00! How much money are these kids raising? (Answer on page 24.)

Conservation and Me

By Kerissa Nelson

Hi! My name is Kerissa Nelson, and in 2005, I won the Junior Duck Stamp Contest. I got some pretty cool prizes for winning ($5,000.00 and a trip to Washington, D.C.), but my favorite prize of all was the internship that I earned with the U.S. Fish & Wildlife Service. By working with this agency these last couple of years, I've learned so much about hunting and conservation and why it is so important that we all get involved.

My entire life I've been a hunter, fisher, and nature lover. When I started working with the U.S. Fish & Wildlife Service in 2006, I learned that I had been a conservationist all this time, too, and I didn't even know it! The earth is an awesome place, and it's our job, even as kids, to contribute to its well-being.

Here's How I Practice Conservation:

I hunt and fish. Every year I buy licenses to hunt and fish. That way I do my part to prevent overpopulation of animals and fish, and I have fun doing it. Can you imagine what the earth would be like if no one went hunting? Animals would make babies like crazy and keep reproducing. They would eat all the food and then go hungry. By buying a license, you're helping to pay for wildlife management.

I buy duck stamps. Before I go hunting, I buy a duck stamp. Money from duck stamps helps support wetlands so that all kinds of fish and wildlife have a home.

By doing these things, I'm doing my part to make sure that all wild animals have the protection they need to survive, and the best part is that I'm having fun doing it. The biggest thing I've learned from working with the U.S. Fish & Wildlife Service is that we can help the

Kerissa and Senator Russ Feingold.

environment and ourselves. For example, when you buy a duck stamp, you help support wetlands; when you shoot your limit that day, you're having grilled duck for dinner.

I encourage others to get involved in the Junior Duck Stamp Program, either through their school or on their own. It's not only fun; it can open doors for you. Look where it has taken me! Oh, and did I mention that's me accepting the award from Senator Russ Feingold?

To learn more about the Junior Duck Stamp Program, visit www.fws.gov/juniorduck/ or www.caljrduckstamp.org. For tips on drawing, contact your local waterfowl association or CWA at www.calwaterfowl.org. Get your school involved! The Web sites are full of information about how to participate.

Imagine, you, too, could help raise $122,500 for conservation!

Becoming a Jake

Ever want to go turkey hunting? You can, thanks mainly to the National Wild Turkey Federation and federal and state wildlife agencies. Back in the 1930s, wild turkeys had almost disappeared in the United States. Thanks to hunters and the National Wild Turkey Federation, we now have over seven million wild turkeys.

Did You Know . . .

- Wild turkeys are very different from their domestic cousins. Domestic and wild turkeys look different. Only wild turkeys can survive in the wild.
- Wild turkeys are big. Adult males, called "gobblers," can stand over three feet tall and weigh over thirty pounds.
- A gobbler's head can change colors—from red to white to blue, depending on its mood.
- Wild turkeys are fast. They can fly up to thirty-five miles per hour.
- Wild turkeys have 5,000 to 6,000 feathers.

In addition to restoring wild turkey populations, the NWTF is dedicated to getting youths involved in hunting, wildlife conservation, and responsible sportsmanship through their JAKES Programs.

JAKES stands for Juniors Acquiring Knowledge, Ethics, and Sportsmanship. The program offers hundreds of fun events throughout the United States each year that involve fishing, camping, and hunting. Of course, you'll even learn how to call in turkeys! Go to www.nwtf.org/jakes and click on "special events" to find a JAKES Conservation Field Day near you!

The NWTF has over half a million members and is located in 50 states. It has raised over $279 million and has spent that money restoring turkey habitat.

Once the habitat is restored, wild turkeys are often released to increase their populations.

Seven Bucks Can Buy a Lot of Fun

Becoming a JAKES member is not just about turkeys. It's about wildlife conservation, backyard ecology, activities (even extreme ones such as kiteboarding), hunting shows for kids, and more.

Test your shooting skills to see how much you know about turkeys at www.nwtf.org. Click on "JAKES" and "Xtreme JAKES," then click on "Fun and Games."

Good Luck!

To become a JAKES member, call 1-800-843-6983
or join online at www.nwtf.org

4-H
Shooting Sports

18 USC 707

The 4-H Shooting Sports Program is a great way to learn about firearms, especially if you do not live in a "hunting area." This program is offered in 46 states. Check out the state by state listings in the back to find programs in your state.

Top Ten Reasons
to Join 4-H Shooting Sports:

1) Are you not very athletic? No need to run fast or jump high here!
2) Some sports are indoors, some outdoors. Some winter, some summer. This is both.
3) In some sports, you may just sit on the bench. Only the good players play. Everyone participates in this sport.
4) It's for boys and girls!
5) No previous experience is required. It's very possible to start as a junior in high school and compete nationally before college.
6) It's a major Olympic event.
7) It doesn't require a team, although you may participate in a team if you wish.
8) In most sports, there is a chance of serious injury. This is the safest of all!
9) Ever see a fight break out on a sports field? To date, there is no record of such bad behavior in this sport. Sportsmanship is highly valued.
10) It pays to play. College scholarships are awarded to both girls and boys!

The 4-H organization originally started as a way to teach farmers' children a new way of farming, but today it is so much more. The 4-H Shooting Sports Program offers not only marksmanship and firearm safety but skills for life. Check out where it's taken these kids. . . .

Keegan today.

Meet 4-H Ambassador Keegan Hammond

Hi, my name is Keegan Hammond, and I am a National Shooting Sports Ambassador for 4-H Shooting Sports. I live in Colorado, and I am the first-ever national ambassador from my state. When I was in middle school, someone encouraged me to join 4-H Shooting Sports.

Sure, I had been hunting for quite some time, but I was extremely shy, and I was the only girl in the program. To make matters worse, everyone seemed to be a better shot than I was. But over the past seven years, I've not only become an excellent shooter, but my life skills have been polished as well.

Perhaps the most important life skill that Shooting Sports has taught me is self-confidence. I participated in my first local youth competition when I was in middle school, but it was not long before my 4-H leaders encouraged me to compete among adults in trapshooting. That is all it took—encouragement to perfect my skills and get further involved in 4-H. I was then chosen by 4-H to become one of its state ambassadors. Imagine, representing the state of Colorado as a Shooting Sports ambassador. I was thrilled! I didn't think it could get much better, but it did.

As the state ambassador, I was chosen to compete at the nationals in Rapid City, South Dakota. Only four kids were invited from across the United States, and I was one of them. This was the competition to become a national ambassador, and even though I was nervous, my training with 4-H had taught me self-confidence and so much more. I spent five days interviewing, doing speeches, filming commercials, doing radio interviews, and meeting with donors—all skills a national ambassador must have. After it was all over, I was chosen as the new National Shooting Sports Ambassador.

So that's my story. Hunting and Shooting Sports have brought so much joy and so many skills into my life. I have always enjoyed hunting, regardless of whether I actually got to shoot something on a particular day; just being outdoors is a big adventure in itself. I always try to pass on gun safety, hunting and shooting tips, and habitat preservation and conservation ideas to other kids so that they, too, may want to experience all that I have.

So get involved and pass it on! Shoot straight and see where it will take you. It's taken me places I never dreamed I would go!

My first bull's-eye.

Meet 4-H Ambassador Justine McQueary

My name is Justine McQueary, and I, too, am a National Shooting Sports Ambassador. Like Keegan, I went through many competitions and have spent hours practicing the sport I love and the skills I have learned. My story, however, is a little different.

Where I grew up, we did not hunt and I had not been around guns. When I was nine years old, my family encouraged me to join the 4-H Shooting Sports Program. What? Me? I was a total girly girl and had never even touched a gun. With some encouragement, I went to a 4-H Shooting Sports practice, and that was it. I was hooked. I wanted

the kind of self-confidence and knowledge that the other kids had, and it looked like way too much fun!

The program began with safety, safety, safety. This issue was made very clear to us: That out of everything we do, safety is always first. I then learned about the basic functions of the guns. Once I had mastered these concepts, I was allowed to shoot. It was a blast.

The 4-H Shooting Sports Program has taught me so much: self confidence, responsibility, concentration, and discipline. As an ambassador, it is my commitment to promote the shooting sports not only in my community and state, but also throughout the United States. As I do this, I see many kids who are young yet are so responsible. These are young 4-H'ers. I also see ones who were just like me, perhaps eight or nine years old and just starting. They're sometimes a bit scared and unsure of themselves. I always stop to share with them my story . . . hey, if a girly girl like me could turn out to be a national ambassador, who knows what they might achieve!

Check out a 4-H shooting clinic in your area at
www.4-hshootingsports.org.

Pheasants Forever and Quail Forever

(and ever and ever)

Hunting upland game is exciting, yet like many of our wild animals, upland game has been affected by the urbanization of our land and loss of good habitat. Years ago, small farms were spread across the United States. These small farms often had open land with native grasses around them, which created perfect homes for pheasants and quail. But today, open grasslands are harder to find. The farms of today are often huge "corporate" farms, and every section is used for farming, leaving little for wildlife.

There's protection in numbers! Because quail are so small, they live in groups called coveys. This helps them stay warm in the winter and provides many eyes to look for danger.

Did you know that pheasants are not native to the United States? They were brought here in 1881 by Judge Owen Nickerson Denny who had just 30 birds shipped here from China. They arrived at his home in Oregon and adapted very well. Just 11 years later, Oregon had its first pheasant hunt (for 75 days) and hunters bagged over 50,000 birds. After that, they were released in 40 of the 50 states.

But the people at Pheasants Forever and Quail Forever are working to change that. By studying pheasant and quail, they learned two important things:

- Pheasant and quail thrive in farmland areas with ample grass. They often live in the same areas, so by restoring habitat for one, both birds are often helped.
- Pheasant and quail do not migrate. They stay in one area throughout their entire lives. Because of that, their homes must offer food, shelter, and protection from predators all year long.

Keeping these facts in mind, Pheasants Forever and Quail Forever have set up local chapters across the United States dedicated to improving habitat. They encourage farmers—both small and large "corporate" ones—to plant native plants next to their fields and surrounding areas. This gives pheasant and quail a habitat to live in. These chapters often have exciting opportunities for youth to get involved in hunting, restoration, and fundraising. Check out what it has offered this gal. . . .

Youth Leadership Council Member Ashley Bishop

Hi! My name is Ashley Bishop. I am from Litchfield, Illinois, and I am now 17 years old. My journey with Pheasants Forever and Quail Forever started when I was just 6. My dad had started our local chapter of Pheasants Forever (PF), and I began by just giving him some pointers on the computer. By helping him, I learned of the important steps that he and our local group (our chapter) were doing to ensure the survival of pheasants in our area. It really opened my eyes to the connection between hunting, conservation, and wildlife habitat restoration.

That was eleven years ago and so much has happened since then. For one, our chapter has grown, and we now have over 100 kids in it. I have also made a lot of new friends. It's neat to have something in common with other kids, and for us it was hunting or working with the adults in habitat restoration. Our chapter worked with many people in the local farming community, showing them ways to make their farms "pheasant friendly."

And I learned how important it is for kids to understand and care about their environment. Sometimes it is the small things,

like planting wildflowers, that attract pheasants to your land. Young people need to learn how to manage and take care of the land properly so that it will benefit not only people but wildlife, too.

When I was 6, I never dreamed I would become so involved in Pheasants Forever. Today I am the president of the National Youth Leadership Council (NYLC). This is a group of kids from across the United States who have been picked for their leadership abilities and their interest in conservation, habitat conservation, and hunting. It has opened many doors for me: I've attended the national convention (where I met the other council members and was elected president) and I even appeared on an episode of Pheasants Forever television, which was shown on the Outdoor Life Network. I've had so much fun, met a lot of incredible kids, and have made many lasting friendships. I encourage all kids to get involved in Pheasants Forever; it has something for everyone!

Check out Ashley and other council members at www.uplandtales. org. Then click on "youth leadership council." You can also view past issues of *Upland Tales* and learn about our native wildlife.

To find a local chapter in your area, go to www.pheasantsforever. com. Then click on the tab to the left that says "local chapters." You'll find a link for Quail Forever on that page as well.

Pheasants Forever has established over 100,000 acres of land for pheasant habitat.

Duke Relax, We're Almost There

Imagine yourself sitting in the backseat of a four-door truck; your buddy is seated up front; and his dad is driving. You've packed the truck with your guns, ammo, ear protection, and everything you need for an afternoon hunt, but all you can think about is "Duke, relax." Sitting next to you is Old Duke, a dog in a crate so excited that the crate is rocking back and forth.

When you arrive at a large, open field, you prepare yourself for the hunt and discuss your hunting plan with the others. Once ready, your buddy goes to let Old Duke out of his crate. You take cover on the other side of the truck, for you are sure that the overly excited dog is going to barrel you over, but surprisingly he does not. Instead, he runs around a bit, nose to the ground, intent on smelling everything in his path. He's on a mission, and, lucky for you, you're not a part of it. Soon Duke settles down and sits next to your buddy, looking for the signal that you are ready to hunt.

The three of you take off walking across the field, with Duke ahead of you and zigzagging across the field at a fast trot. His nose is again on the ground when suddenly he stops and freezes in place like a statue. As you approach the dog, you see nothing except tall grass, but Duke is never wrong. He's found your game. Do you know what you are hunting for?

This dog is pointing out game to the hunter.

It's Your First Upland Game Hunt and Duke's Done a Fine Job!

The word upland game refers to birds like pheasants, chukar, Hungarian partridge, quail, and others. Unlike ducks, these birds don't migrate but, instead, live in permanent territories or homes. Often these homes are large open fields covered in tall grass or brush. You may be used to seeing birds in trees, but these birds spend the majority of their time on the ground. When they feel threatened, they hold completely still while hiding in the grass or brush. That is why we brought Old Duke, for he will find the birds for us.

Half of the fun of hunting upland game is watching a dog find a bird. Hunting dogs have been bred specifically for the type of game they are hunting. Some are good swimmers and specialize in waterfowl; others like beagles may hunt fox. Upland game dogs are generally pointers, and just like the name suggests, their job is to point out the birds for you. You don't have to have a dog to shoot upland game; it just makes it more fun.

Good boy . . . Once the bird flushes (flies up) and is shot, the dog retrieves the bird and brings it back to the hunter.

Safari Club International

For many nonhunters and even some bird hunters, the thought of big-game hunting brings up a sour taste in their mouths. After all, big-game hunters are those heartless people who wander the earth's natural wildernesses, shooting down majestic animals and placing them in danger of extinction. Nothing could be further from the truth ... and organizations like Safari Club International are an excellent example of the contributions big-game hunters make in the conservation and survival of our world's wildlife.

Safari Club International (SCI), an international organization of big-game hunters, is recognized as a leader in wildlife conservation. Its members are people who shoot big game in Africa, Asia, North America, and around the world. They may shoot elephants, zebra, deer, leopard, or buffalo, and your first thought may be that this is bad. But we're going to take a closer look at the contributions of the big-game hunter and how organizations like SCI benefit our world's wildlife.

Let's look at Africa. You've most likely seen a television program about African wildlife. It was probably filmed in a national park like the Serengeti where wildlife is protected, as it should be. These reserves, which allow animals to roam safely, also benefit people. Tourists are able to view wildlife, scientists can study them, and we can learn about the needs of the various species to aid in their survival.

We know that animals migrate in and out of the parks, so how can we keep them safe from poachers, and how do big-game hunters help protect African wildlife? Do you know the answer to the question on the next page?

Is It Fact or Is It Fiction?
(Let's find out)

By allowing big-game hunters to hunt outside of the parks in Africa, animals will not be able to reach the safety of the park, so populations will dwindle, eventually causing the various species to become threatened or endangered.

This is entirely false, and there are several reasons why. Just like in the United States, big-game hunters must buy a license for each animal he wants to hunt, and he is allowed to shoot only certain species. His license also tells him how many he can shoot. For example, he might be able to shoot two warthogs but he'll be able to shoot only one lion. (The various African countries where it is legal to hunt manage wildlife just like we do.) In Africa, a hunter must also pay a trophy fee to the government for each animal he has shot.

This African game hunter is accompanied by locally employed guides as well as an African game warden. African game wardens often accompany hunters, making sure all the rules of hunting are followed.

In order to sustain the wildlife populations in a country, the money collected for license and trophy fees goes to the government to help pay for wildlife management; some of the money also goes to the local inhabitants who help protect the wildlife in their area. The government designates which areas can be used for hunting, and it sells the right to hunt in these areas to professional hunting companies. It is these companies who arrange safaris and provide professional hunters to guide you on your hunt. Each government also makes strict rules on all aspects of hunting with a firearm or bow. These regulations help protect the wildlife and ensure the survival of the many species found in each country.

Because hunting companies buy the right to hunt in a particular area, they are very concerned about keeping illegal hunters out. These illegal hunters are called poachers. Hunting companies often provide antipoaching patrols to protect the animals in their areas. Without antipoaching patrols, the result would be devastating: Without protection, many animals would be killed for food, horns, or ivory.

In Africa both people and animals compete for land. Thus, by allowing big-game hunters to buy licenses and hunt, some of the money and all the meat go to the local people, while the hunting company provides protection to many animals that the government cannot. Both people and animals benefit.

It's a WIN-WIN situation. These hunters have just shot a Cape buffalo in Zambia. The man in the middle is the local chief of a nearby village. Even though the hunters shot a buffalo, the meat does not belong to them. The law requires that foreign hunters donate the animal to the chief, who in turn provides his people with the meat. By doing this, the local people are less likely to poach animals for food, and the fees that the hunters paid to shoot the animal go to the government. A pretty nifty arrangement!

Do People Still Hunt African Elephants?
Yes, they do, but they must do it legally.

Legal Hunting of Elephants

In some countries in Africa, there are too many elephants, so sometimes it is necessary to kill a certain number, or there would be no place for people to live or enough food for the elephants. Each country, therefore, sets a quota of how many elephant licenses it will sell each year. Hunters must pay for the license to shoot an elephant, and, once an elephant is shot, the hunter must pay a trophy fee. The license costs as much as $10,000 or more. This money goes to the government, which in turn uses it to protect the wildlife and support the local economy.

Hunters who have shot elephants legally can bring the ivory into the United States under controlled situations and with the proper legal permits. However, they cannot sell any portion of the elephant, including the ivory. The meat is always given to the local villages.

Illegal Hunting of Elephants

It is illegal to hunt an elephant without obtaining a license first. Illegal hunting is called poaching. Just like the market hunting of the American buffalo, market hunters seeking ivory nearly wiped out the elephant population years ago. Strict regulations now protect elephants from this type of hunting. It is illegal to sell ivory, even if it is obtained by a hunter who shot his elephant legally.

Organizations like Safari Club International do much more around the globe than just support big-game hunting. They invest millions of dollars each year into conservation programs. Whether it is relocating moose to Michigan, building blue bird boxes (manmade nests) in New York, or purchasing conservation easements for jaguars in Mexico, Safari Club International is truly making a huge contribution to the survival of animals around the world.

SCI also invests in educational programs for kids and young adults. By educating kids, SCI is investing in a new generation of hunters and conservationists. SCI believes that's important. By becoming involved in conservation projects, kids are reaching out across the United States and around the world, and by learning about hunting, hunter safety, firearms, and game animals, kids will perpetuate the sport of big-game hunting for future generations.

Send Your Teacher to School

That's right, while you are on summer vacation, you can send your teacher to the American Wilderness Leadership School in Wyoming. This is a special school for teachers run by Safari Club International. Your teacher will learn about native wildlife, conservation projects, wetlands, archery, fishing, hunting, firearms, and how wildlife is managed throughout the United States. They will learn current environmental issues and how to involve their students in outdoor life. The best part is that they will return home with their hands full of projects that will get their students involved in conservation and the big outdoors. And it doesn't matter what grade you are in. It's for teachers of all grade levels. Check out the American Wilderness Leadership School by going to www.safariclubfoundation.org

SAFARI IN A BOX

So you don't have a teacher that can go to the American Wilderness Leadership School? Well, no worries. Safari Club International will come to your school, in a box. The Safari in A Box Program is designed to give you a hands-on wildlife experience even if you live in the city. It's a kit that teaches you about animals that live right here in the United States, and it is full of lesson plans, fun activity suggestions, teachers' guides, real or replica skulls, pelts, repliscat (that's fake poop), and rubber tracks to help you learn about our native wildlife.

Learn more about the Safari in A Box Program by going to www.safariclubfoundation.org, then click on "Sables" on the left-hand side.

Hint: Your local chapter of Safari Club International is one of the best ways to find out what Safari Club has to offer in your area. SCI also, at times, will pay for part or all of the cost to send your teacher to its leadership school, and it will help your teacher purchase the Safari in A Box kit for your school. To find a local chapter, go to www.safariclub.org, click on "Chapters" on the left. You can also find one by calling (888) 553-5838.

The National Rifle Association

With so many options and ways to get involved in shooting sports, it's nice to know that there is one BIG organization that can help. Located in all fifty states, the National Rifle Association (NRA) is dedicated to promoting the shooting sports for all Americans, including today's youth.

In 1871 the NRA was formed. Its main goal was to provide a shooting range where individuals could practice their marksmanship. In 1903 the NRA promoted the establishment of rifle clubs at all major colleges, universities, and military academies. By 1906 it had created youth shooting programs, and today, over one hundred years later, more than one million youth participate annually in NRA shooting sports events and in programs sponsored by the NRA.

Like big-game hunters and shooters, the NRA is often misunderstood. Some people think the NRA is simply an organization that promotes gun use throughout the United States, regardless of how the guns are actually used. This is not true. We all know that it's a bad thing to put guns in the hands of criminals or the mentally disturbed. The NRA knows this, too. Before we look into how the NRA can help you get involved in hunting, firearm safety, and conservation, let's look at why the NRA is an important organization in our society, especially today.

A Bit of History
(just a small bit)

If you have studied United States history in school, you may be familiar with the Bill of Rights. The Bill of Rights contains the first ten amendments to the Constitution; it was introduced in 1789 by James Madison and became law in 1791. It is the part of the law that gives you individual rights as a citizen of the United States; these rights include freedom of speech, the right to choose your own religion, and the right to keep and bear arms (that is the right to own a firearm). The Bill of Rights limits the powers of the federal government, it prohibits cruel or unusual punishments, and it protects a person's right to life, liberty, and property. The Bill of Rights defines the freedoms we have as citizens of the United States.

With these rights come responsibility. We have the right to freedom of speech, but that does not mean we should be rude or disrespectful of others. We have the right to bear arms, but that does not mean we can act irresponsibly. As citizens, we are entitled to all our rights. But it is our duty to act in a responsible manner.

Eddie the Eagle
and Gun Responsibility

Since 1988, Eddie the Eagle has spoken to twenty-one million children in all fifty states. He talks to kids in pre-school to third grade. His message is simple and easy to remember:

Does this have anything to do with hunting and conservation? The answer is NO. We've included Eddie into this book because we think Eddie the Eagle is way cool. Every kid, parent, teacher, and community leader should know about him. Check him out and pass the word!

If you see a gun:

STOP!
Don't Touch
Leave the Area
Tell an Adult

Eddie does not teach whether guns are good or bad; his only goal is to help protect children and keep them safe. We think gun safety is an important message for all children. Teaching gun safety is kind of like teaching children about the danger of swimming pools. You may not have a pool, but what if your neighbor does? In the same sense, you may not have a gun in your house, but what if your neighbor does? Eddie teaches young children what to do if they see a gun. Way to go, Eddie!

The Top Ten Reasons to Have the Eddie the Eagle Gun Safe® Program at Your School

1. Nearly one half of all Americans have some type of firearm in their household. Just as it is important for kids to know not to play in the street, kids need to know what to do if they see a gun. Eddie's rules are simple.
2. They can be taught in a one-day format or a five-day format; the choice is yours.
3. Eddie provides student workbooks, an animated video, and instructor guides.
4. Kids need to understand that the guns they see on television or in cartoons are not real. Even though people get up after getting shot on T.V., kids need to know that the programs are make-believe and guns can kill. In real life, and in all cases, kids must follow Eddie's rules when they come across a firearm.
5. Programs are available in both English and Spanish.
6. Eddie is not shown touching a firearm, and does not promote firearm use or ownership.
7. Eddie has no hidden agenda. He never mentions the NRA.
8. The program is available for a small fee, and can be taught over and over again to new students.
9. Students get reward stickers for attending the class.
10. Anyone can teach the Eddie the Eagle program with help from the NRA.

We give Eddie a big two thumbs up for keeping our kids safe.
To find an Eddie the Eagle Gun Safe® Program near you, contact the NRA at 1(800) 231-0752 or eddie@nrahq.org.
Now, back to how the NRA can help you. . . .

Finding Your Way through the NRA

Start here: www.nrahq.org/youth/

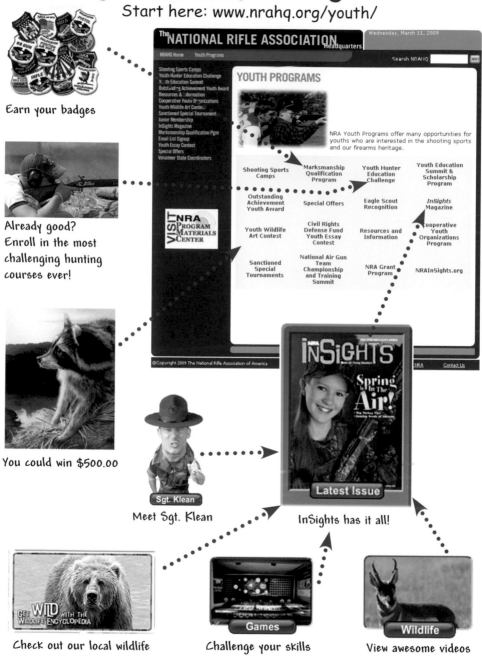

Earn your badges

Already good?
Enroll in the most
challenging hunting
courses ever!

You could win $500.00

Meet Sgt. Klean

InSights has it all!

Check out our local wildlife

Challenge your skills

View awesome videos

If you don't have a computer with access to the Internet, get involved
with the NRA Youth Programs by subscribing to *InSights* magazine (to get
all the cool news) by calling: Toll free 1-800-672-3888

Meet Hot Shot
Jon Michael McGrath II

Hi. My name is Jon Michael McGrath II. I am 16 years old and a junior at Bishop Kelley High School in Tulsa, Oklahoma. Many people say I have an incredible story to share, being one of the youngest members of the United States Shooting Team (those are the people who compete at the Olympics). I shoot here in the U.S. as well as overseas. I was representing the United States in competitions before I was old enough to even drive. Here is my story.

When I was 11 years old, I attended a summer Boy Scout camp in Oklahoma. On one of the free days at camp, you could participate in any activity you desired. I had a small BB gun at home, which my dad had taught me to use, but I had never shot a shotgun. There were no other kids in line at the shotgun station, so that is what I chose. The instructor gave me the proper ear and eye protection and then instructed me on the rules for safety. Once I was ready, the clay targets were released, and I hit one, then another, and another and another. I hit almost all of them. The range master turned around and told my dad, "Hey, this kid is pretty good. You should get him involved in the shooting sports."

The following week, I took my first lesson at the Tulsa Gun Club. The first thing I learned was safety and how to handle a firearm properly. After that, I was allowed to shoot on the skeet field. Skeet is a type of shooting competition where you stand on a semicircular field. There are 8 stations that the shooter stands at and clay targets are thrown across the field. My first time

Photo by Steve Wagner and courtesy of National Shooting Sports Foundation.

Four months after I first picked up a shotgun at Boy Scout camp, I won a gold medal competing against adults.

to shoot, I hit 20 out of 25 targets. That's a pretty good score since the average is about 11.

I continued to go to the range to take lessons, and I continued to improve. Some of the people at the range were going to the National Skeet Shooting Association World Skeet Championship in Texas. They told me that if I could hit 95 out of 100 clay targets, they would let me shoot on their squad at the World Championship. I practiced and practiced and hit that mark. Yes, I was going to Texas! You could not imagine how excited I was to go. It had only been four months since I first picked up a shotgun at Boy Scout camp, and now I was going to the National Shooting Complex in San Antonio, Texas. But it just got better and better. During the competition, it was raining on and off all day, but I didn't let that bother me. I just got out there and did my best. In the first event I hit 98 out of 100 targets. When it came to the main event in 12-gauge, I shot 122 out of 125 targets and won a gold medal competing against adults. I was only 11 at the time.

When I returned home, I continued to practice and improve. I joined 4-H Shooting Sports and continued in Boy Scouts. The following year when I was 12, I attended my first Junior World Skeet Championship. I was a bit nervous because I was not a very big kid, and the kids I was competing against were older and some were even over 6 feet tall. But I had learned through Boy Scouts to always do my best, and that was what I was going to do. All of the sudden, I was tied for the overall high score. Then it happened in a shoot-off. I hit all my targets and won the

Junior World Championship title and a gold medal! The following January, I was named captain of the Sub-Junior All American Skeet Team. I was 12 years old and the youngest All America Athlete in the country.

The year following my Junior World Championship Title, at age 13 I decided that I wanted to try International Skeet. It's a little different than American Skeet and a bit faster. I went out to the U.S. Olympic Training Center in Colorado Springs, the home of the USA Shotgun Team. The International Shooting Park is surrounded by some of the most beautiful mountains in the country; it is breathtaking.

I arrived just a few days before the Junior Olympic Championships. I did OK in practice but when the competition came around, I couldn't hit a thing. One of my scores was 9 out of 25. If I was going to make a go of this, I was going to have to practice and learn more about it. I wanted to return and compete for the Olympic Team the following year, so I made it a priority to improve my skills. I joined the Scholastic Clay Target Program (SCTP) and shot on the National Skeet Shooting Association circuit all over the country. When the time came the following year to return to Colorado, I was not going to let that range get the best of me. I jumped out and never looked back, right through the match finals. I had won my first National Championship in International Skeet.

Look closely. Jon Michael is practicing "skeet." The arrows show his target and the shot in motion.

At age 16, Jon Michael competes as part of the USA National Shooting Team. (Photo by Craig Hancock)

In 2007, the first round of U.S. Olympic Trials began. During my first trial, my scores were not the best. I placed 10th. The next trials would come up in spring of 2008, and I was determined to be more prepared and I was. I placed 4th, which put me in line as an alternate shooter at the 2008 Olympic Games in Beijing, China. My trip to China was an experience like no other. To be surrounded by the world's top athletes and to be part of the USA Shooting Team is an honor that I take very seriously. I am so proud to be a part of it, and the men and women who represent the USA are all first class and excellent role models on and off the field.

I went from a kid who shot his first shotgun at Boy Scout camp at age 11 . . . to being a member of the United States Shooting Team at age 16. When people say that the Shooting Sports can take you places, believe them!

Today, I still compete here in the U.S. and also overseas as part of the USA Shooting Team. I am also a national ambassador for the Scholastic Clay Target Program in which I help promote the shooting sports around the country. I speak to thousands of kids each year to help them get involved.

There are a number of places that can help you get started: Boy Scouts, the Scholastic Clay Target Program, 4-H, Civilian Marksmanship Programs, and others. The National Rifle Association has been very supportive in my shooting career and has excellent shooting programs for youth.

The shooting sports in the U.S. provide our youth with experiences that you would not normally encounter, and it opens doors of opportunity for you. It is also a sport that you can participate in throughout your entire life. You can receive a college education and even represent your country overseas. The sky is the limit. It is amazing what happens when you give it your all.

To see where Jon Michael McGrath II is going next and to track his progress, log on to www.JonMichaelMcGrath.com

.... News Flash ....

Believe It or Not

Since his return from the Olympics,
Jon Michael has won a gold medal and
the title of World Champion in the open division of
the 2009 NSSA International World Skeet Championship.
And just to top that, he has broken
three world records in shooting!

(Yes, you can believe it, and there is no stopping him now!)

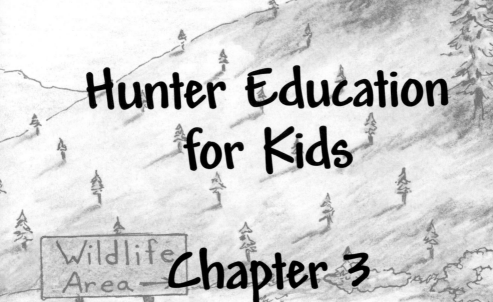

Hunter Education
for Kids

Chapter 3

It all begins here!

Don't Be a Dummy

So you're all hyped up: You want to become a hunter. It looks like those kids are having just too much fun. Let's just grab a gun and go have some fun! WRONG! STOP RIGHT THERE! It's not only dangerous . . . it's illegal!

Hunting and shooting sports are loads of fun, but they are extremely dangerous if you have not had proper training and supervision. So before engaging in any hunting activity, you'll need to take a hunter safety/education course. These courses are offered by various organizations, but we recommend that you contact your state wildlife agency and enroll in one of their standardized courses. Their programs are designed for youth and are required if you want to get a hunting license. The more you know, the more comfortable you'll be, and you'll become not only a safe hunter but also a more successful one.

Kids attend a state sponsored hunter-education course.

Learn the correct ammunition so that this doesn't happen to you.

A hunter's education course will teach you the basics of rifles, shotguns, and handguns. You'll learn how to handle each, what makes them unique from each other, the types of ranges (called the effective range) each is capable of, their safety features, and why it is so important to match the correct ammunition to the correct firearm. You'll also learn about muzzleloaders and archery equipment. You'll discover the difference between a bolt action and a break action over-and-under. You'll learn the difference between a 20- and 28-gauge shotgun. You'll be able to discuss what a smoothbore is, and what

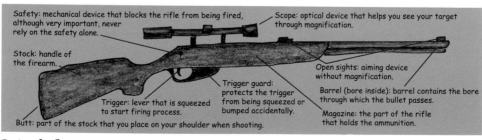

Safety: mechanical device that blocks the rifle from being fired, although very important, never rely on the safety alone.

Scope: optical device that helps you see your target through magnification.

Stock: handle of the firearm.

Trigger guard: protects the trigger from being squeezed or bumped accidentally.

Trigger: lever that is squeezed to start firing process.

Open sights: aiming device without magnification.

Barrel (bore inside): barrel contains the bore through which the bullet passes.

Magazine: the part of the rifle that holds the ammunition.

Butt: part of the stock that you place on your shoulder when shooting.

Parts of rifle.

happens if a hangfire occurs. You will be taught where the safety on a gun is, how to load and unload a gun, and what to do if it jams. The list goes on and on. . . .

To be a good hunter, you need to know how to shoot well. Did you know that you probably have a "master eye"? That's one eye that is dominant over the other. Knowing this and knowing how to use your eyes will make you a better hunter. Basic shooting skills are discussed in a hunter-education class. You will learn the arc that a bullet takes, and you will learn that what you shoot at is not necessarily where the bullet will go! This course will teach you essential knowledge so that you will learn how to shoot accurately.

OK, you think you're ready to hunt, but where's the game? There are still a few lessons to learn. Good hunters must be good shots, but they also need to know about game animals. Good hunters need to learn the fine art of stalking, setting up blinds, and calling in game; good hunters also need to learn the difference between a male and a female for each species they want to hunt. They need to learn where on each animal to place the "vital shot," and they need to know how to field dress game.

Safety is a large part of this course, and it's the most important part. Learn what to do and what not to do when handling guns. The following ten commandments of shooting safety highlight the most important parts of gun safety, but hunter education courses illustrate each of these rules by giving you specific situations so that you can really "see" what happens if you aren't careful. These lessons will stick in your mind forever!

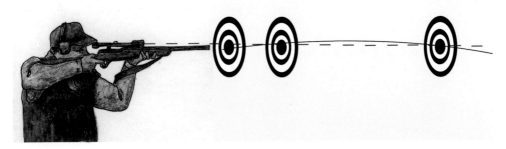

Ten Commandments
of Shooting Safety

1)   Watch that muzzle!

2)   Treat every firearm as if it were loaded.

3)   Be sure of your target, and what is in front of it, and behind it.

4)   Keep your finger outside the trigger guard until you are ready to shoot, and keep the safety on when you're not using the firearm.

5)   Make sure your gun is free of obstructions, and make sure you have the correct ammunition.

6)   Unload firearms when you're not using them.

7)   Never point a firearm at another person, and make sure to point a firearm only at something you intend to shoot.

8)   Don't run, jump, or climb with a firearm.

9)   Store firearms and ammunition separately and safely.

10)   Do not take mind-altering medications or drugs when handling firearms, and never ever drink alcohol when using a loaded gun.

And one more . . . If it's not going on your plate for dinner, don't shoot it!

There are several things wrong with each of these pictures.

Do you know what they are?

(Answers are on the following page.)

In picture #1, the hunter does not know what is beyond the animal. It is "skylined" and a shot would be dangerous, for the bullet could miss or pass through the animal and hit something else, including a person! Also, did you notice the building? It's not only dangerous but illegal to discharge a firearm near a building.

In picture #2, first of all, the animal is again "skylined." We cannot see what is beyond it, and this is especially true for the hunter on the right. Second, two people should never be shooting or aiming at the same target. Third, to make matters even worse, the hunter on the left is behind the hunter on the right, placing him in extreme danger.

Ethical hunting is the second most important thing you'll learn in a hunter-education class. (Safety is first.) So just what is an ethical hunter? An ethical hunter is a hunter who does the right thing when no one is watching . . . even if the wrong thing is legal. Ethical behavior has to do with issues of fairness, respect, and responsibility not covered by laws. For example, it is not illegal to be rude to a landowner after he has given you permission to hunt on his property, but it is discourteous. It is not illegal to strap a dead deer onto your vehicle to transport it home, but it will surely offend nonhunters, so why do it? It's legal in some countries to shoot a caged animal, but it is unethical to do so. Irresponsible and discourteous behavior done by just a few hunters give all hunters a bad name. Good sportsmanship and good behavior ensures our privilege to hunt.

Ethical hunting especially applies to how you treat the animals you are hunting. Let's say you are stalking a deer and the deer gets cornered by a fence. Would you shoot it? The ethical hunter would say, "No, that is not a fair-chase shot." Fair chase is just that, "fair." A buck up against a fence is not fair, for the animal has no chance to escape.

Ethical hunters will walk away from this situation.

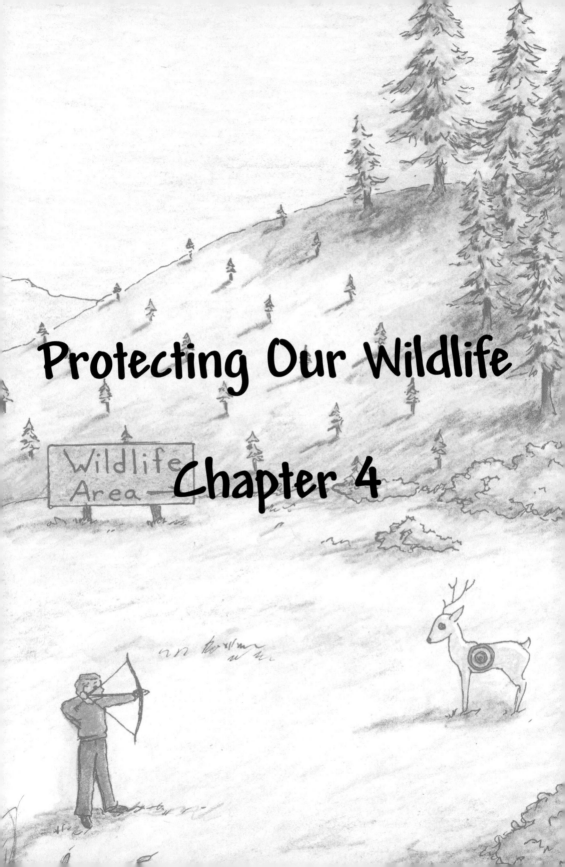

Protecting Our Wildlife

Chapter 4

Wildlife Area

Money spent on hunting goes to support government agencies. They are the "watchdogs" for our wildlife, and we love them!

We're Watching You

The vast majority of today's modern hunters are ethical. They abide by the laws governing hunting and show respect for wildlife and our society as a whole. But like all sections of society, there are a few bad apples. Unethical hunters who shoot at game from cars or planes give hunting a bad name, but there is another group of bad apples that are even worse. The people in this group don't buy licenses, they don't respect the wildlife laws, and they hunt whenever they feel like it. These people are poachers.

Poachers are just like thieves. Poaching is the illegal taking of fish and wildlife. They may shoot game out of season, take more animals than the law allows (including fish), or take animals that are protected by law (like our bald eagle). They may even take animals to sell commercially (like the old buffalo hunters). All these acts are illegal. Poachers are sneaky little devils, too. They operate in secrecy and often at night. Their illegal behavior hurts everyone—you, me, nonhunters—but mostly their behavior hurts our wildlife.

But thanks to our state wildlife agencies and concerned individuals, poachers are hunted down and thrown in jail. To catch a poacher, a game warden must think like a poacher, and state wildlife agencies are

Bobcats are legal to shoot in many states, but shooting them and selling their hides (market hunting) is illegal. These bobcats were shot and skinned by a poacher wanting to sell the skins. But U.S Fish & Game wardens were one step ahead of him. The man pictured above is not the poacher but an undercover game warden. He posed as a purchaser and busted the poacher. Way to go!

good at finding criminals. They catch illegal poachers by watching them through binoculars, by setting up sting operations, by going undercover, and by following up on tips provided by the public.

Here's an example of how game wardens catch poachers: Just as it was getting dark these fishermen headed out to sea off the California coast. They anchored their boat and acted as though they were out to catch sea urchins. But in the distance game wardens were watching them through binoculars. The fishermen were lifting the floorboards of the boat and stashing their catch below. They were obviously hiding something. That's when game wardens moved in to investigate.

Look what was hiding under the floorboards! It's an illegal catch of abalone. The fishermen were arrested immediately.

State wildlife agencies have a lot of other responsibilities besides catching poachers. These are the people who establish your state's hunting regulations. They set hunting seasons and bag limits (like how many ducks you can shoot). As guardians of wildlife, they monitor the animals in your state and determine rules that each hunter must follow.

It's the duty of the state wildlife agency to monitor the population of game species to determine the number of tags* it will issue each year. This will vary, depending on such factors as the number of live animals of each species and conditions of the habitat in which they live. Let's look at the two scenarios for deer below. Can you tell what the game wardens will do in each case?   (*That's the number of deer that can be shot in a season.)

Let's say for several years now the weather has been good and the winters brought a lot of rain. This created lots of food for the deer, and although there were predators around, the deer still multiplied and increased in population. If you said that the state wildlife agency would increase the number of tags, you would be right.

Two years later, the rains stopped. A drought set in, and areas became very dry. Perhaps there were even wildfires that burned the deer's habitat. Food became scarce, and predators were still around and going strong. (Predators, like coyotes, are not affected by lack of vegetation.) The deer population dropped. Many starved to death. What would the state agencies do here?

Deer tags increased

Deer tags decreased

State agency game wardens are highly respected for the work they do for wildlife by both hunters and nonhunters. Game wardens go through extensive training and often work around the clock, including weekends. We give them a big "hats off to you." They bust the bad guys, they guard our wildlife, and they get to work outdoors . . . how cool would this job be!

Game wardens find themselves in all types of situations, like this one who is helping to rescue people lost in the wilderness.

Protecting our wildlife is no easy job. Game wardens are trained to know:
* Firearms and defensive tactics
* Fish and wildlife laws
* How to handle "evidence"
* Search and arrest techniques
* Policies and procedures

To Catch a Thief
(or a poacher)

All states rely on confidential "hotlines" to learn of crimes against wildlife. A listing of your state's hotline can be found on page 76. It's a good number to know. But remember, if you see an animal being poached or know of a crime against wildlife, follow these precautions:

* Never approach a person or group of people committing a crime. This can be dangerous. Play dumb and act as if you don't know the action is illegal. Later, you can tell a trusted adult.
* Make a mental note of what is happening: Is it a man or a woman? What are they wearing? Where did the crime take place (by a stream, group of rocks, etc.)? What type of car were they driving?
* Leave the area immediately and tell a parent or trusted adult what happened. If they wish to report it, give them the number for your state's hotline.

State Hotlines to Report a Poacher

Alabama	800-272-4263		Montana	800-847-6668
Alaska	800-478-3377		Nebraska	800-742-7627
Arizona	800-352-0700		Nevada	800-992-3030
Arkansas	800-482-9262		New Hampshire	800-344-4262
California	888-334-2258		New Jersey	800-222-0456
Colorado	800-332-4155		New Mexico	800-432-4263
Connecticut	800-842-4357		New York	800-847-7332
Delaware	800-292-3030		North Carolina	800-662-7137
Florida	888-404-3922		North Dakota	800-472-2121
Georgia	800-241-4113		Ohio	800-762-2437
Hawaii	808-587-0077		Oklahoma	800-522-8039
Idaho	800-632-5999		Oregon	800-452-7888
Illinois	877-236-7529		Pennsylvania	888-742-8001
Indiana	800-847-4367		Rhode Island	800-498-1336
Iowa	800-532-2020		South Carolina	800-922-5431
Kansas	877-426-3843		South Dakota	800-592-5522
Kentucky	800-252-5378		Tennessee	800-255-8972
Louisiana	800-442-2511		Texas	800-792-4263
Maine	800-253-7887		Utah	800-662-3337
Maryland	800-635-6124		Vermont	800-752-5378
Massachusetts	800-632-8075		Virginia	800-237-5712
Michigan	800-292-7800		Washington	800-477-6224
Minnesota	800-652-9093		West Virginia	800-638-4263
Mississippi	800-237-6278		Wisconsin	800-847-9367
Missouri	800-392-1111		Wyoming	800-442-4331

Wildlife CSI to the Rescue

Along a rural road in the small town of Ashland, Oregon, are two very important buildings. They sit side by side, surrounded by beautiful gardens and tall trees. Inside, some of our most important work for the protection of wildlife is being done.

The talons of an eagle hang on a wall, along with a python skin, an alligator purse, and what looks like ivory. Jars containing gall bladders of bears, turtle eggs, and dead reptiles are on the shelves. A rhino head is in a dark corner with a blue light above it, and a man is carefully inspecting it. The walk-in freezer contains tiger meat, primate parts, and a host of other parts all wrapped carefully and tagged. No, it's not a witches den: It's the National Fish and Wildlife Forensics Laboratory, and it is the only laboratory in the world devoted to wildlife law enforcement. Everything in the lab is evidence from a crime scene.

Photo Courtesy National Fish and Wildlife Forensics Laboratory

This crime lab contains not only animal parts, but high-tech equipment used to solve wildlife crimes. There are about twenty-five scientists working in this lab. It is their job to solve crimes just as police officers and detectives do; however, the crimes they are solving have been committed against animals, not people.

You have probably seen on television shows, such as CSI, how forensics is used to solve crimes. The word forensics actually refers to various investigative sciences that can help answer questions of interest in the legal system. For example, meat all looks the same. You might go to the store and see different cuts of meat, labeled New York, rib-eye, tri-tip, and so on. You naturally assume that this meat all comes from a cow. But other than taste, how would you prove it? It is the job of the National Fish and Wildlife Forensics Lab to identify the species or subspecies of pieces, parts, or products of an animal to determine what it was and its cause of death. The lab is important because it helps wildlife officers determine if a violation of law has occurred, and it identifies and compares physical evidence in an attempt to link suspect, victim, and crime scene.

Reasonable Doubt

In order to prosecute a criminal, our justice system requires that guilt be established "beyond a reasonable doubt." There are two ways to do this:

1) Have an eyewitness—someone who actually saw the crime being committed.
2) Have physical evidence such as the body or parts of the body of the animal that was killed.

But connecting the body part to an actual animal or person is difficult. This is where the sleuths at the Wildlife Forensics Lab step in.

The Case of the Ivory Smuggler

In 2004 the Wildlife Forensics Lab received a package from U.S. Fish & Wildlife agents. Inside they found photographs and samples of what appeared to be ivory products (elephant tusks are made of ivory). It also contained a report asking the forensics lab to identify the material in the products.

Photo Courtesy National Fish and Wildlife Forensics Laboratory

Elephant ivory can be carved into many shapes and forms.

The U.S. Fish & Wildlife agents had confiscated these products at a port. These items had been shipped to the United States by a woman who claimed they were made of mammoth tusks, not modern-day elephant tusks. Mammoths, distant cousins to our elephants of today, became extinct over ten thousand years ago. Selling mammoth ivory is legal; selling modern-day elephant ivory is not. The agents suspected that this woman was not telling the truth, and they asked the forensics lab to prove it.

First the scientists at the lab had to determine that these products were indeed ivory and not plastic. An ultraviolet light found the mineral apatite in the products, a component of bone and ivory but not of plastic. Second, by using a microscope, the scientists determined that the ivory was that of an African elephant and not an Asian one.

Photo Courtesy of National Fish & Wildlife Forensics Laboratory

Next came the tough part. The agents knew they had ivory of an African elephant, but was it a modern-day elephant or was it ivory from an extinct

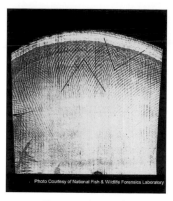
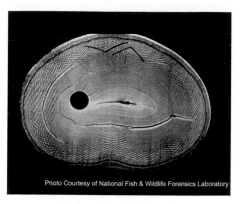

Extinct mammoth   Modern day elephant

mammoth, an animal that roamed the earth 10,000 years ago? This was tough to answer for there was no book, no manual, and no Internet site that had the answer. They would have to figure it out for themselves.

With nowhere else to go, they started to look at small pieces of both elephant ivory and mammoth ivory. Somehow, they would have to find a way to tell them apart. The answer came to them when they compared the very small lines found on the tusks of both modern-day elephants and mammoths. Because the lines are tiny and hard to see, they placed the ivory on a photocopy machine and made enlarged images of it. By measuring the angles where the lines crossed (called Schreger lines), they found that these angles were different in both subspecies. They found that the Schreger lines in modern-day elephants were wider than those found in the ivory of mammoths.

Once they found a way to determine the differences in ivory, they returned to the ivory products shipped to them. The U.S. Fish & Wildlife agents were right: The products they had questioned were not made from ancient mammoth tusks but were from modern-day elephants—these elephants had been illegally shot and killed. The good work of the forensics lab was used to help prosecute this woman. She pleaded guilty and received a sentence of five years in prison and a $100,000 fine.

We are lucky to have such a wonderful lab and dedicated scientists to help protect our wildlife. It is also important to note that this lab is supported by contributions from hunters and hunting organizations throughout the United States.

Was a Crime Committed?

Only the forensics lab will know for sure. These technicians are in the process of determining what killed these animals. Perhaps they were hit by a car, shot, poisoned, or died of natural causes. Whatever the reason, the sleuths at the forensics lab will find it.

Photo Courtesy of National Fish and Wildlife Forensics Laboratory

A Strange but True Tale

In Illinois, agents came across a butcher who was selling lion meat. (Why would anyone want to sell lion meat and who would want to eat it?) Although lions are not endangered and, therefore, the meat is legal to sell, the folks at Fish & Wildlife were suspicious. Was it really lion meat? Since they could not tell by looking at it or tasting it, they bought some and sent it to the lab in Oregon.

Photo Courtesy National Fish and Wildlife Forensics Laboratory

Here the lab did a series of DNA tests, and, sure enough, it was not lion meat, but the meat of the endangered tiger. Without this type of crime lab for animals, this case would never have been solved.

Hunters Make a Difference

Chapter 5

Wildlife Area

Hunting Economics 101

Ever wonder what the world would be like without hunters? For our wildlife it wouldn't be very pretty. Let's see. . . . First off, without hunters we would not have hunting organizations (like the ones you just read about) that put conservation of wildlife first. There would be a lot less money going to support our wildlife, enrich habitat, and provide conservation programs. And all those people who work for those organizations, well, they'd have to get another job. But how about the individual hunter? It is through the fees charged to individual hunters that we pay for much of our conservation, game wardens, and wildlife services. Hummm . . . Let's look at just one year, the year 2007, to get an idea of how much individual hunters contribute to the benefit of wildlife and conservation.

The Year 2007

723 million dollars

That's the amount of money that was collected from the sales of state hunting licenses, tags, and permits across the United States.

25 million dollars

That was the amount of money collected from the purchase of Federal Duck Stamps.

266 million dollars

This amount of money (an 11 percent tax) was collected from hunters when they purchased certain hunting supplies such as guns or ammunition. It's a special tax called an excise tax that only sportsmen pay when they purchase certain items. The tax was created in 1937, and the money collected from it supports wildlife management, hunter-education programs, and shooting-range development. In fact, since it was created, this tax has distributed over 3.8 billion dollars to state wildlife agencies.

Our economy also benefits from hunters. With 147 million hunters in the United States, just imagine all the jobs and all the money they provide. For many hunters, having all the "stuff" that goes with hunting is almost as fun as hunting itself. For example, hunters purchase camo jackets, camo hats, boots, tents, duck calls, decoys, ammo, turkey calls, guns, face paint . . . the list goes on and on. It's almost as much fun to go into a good hunting store just to look around as it is to go hunting.

Let's look at just one hunter. It's the start of duck season, and this hunter (we'll call him Jim) wants to go hunting. He needs a license and he needs a new pair of waders, so he heads to his favorite hunting store. We'll follow along.

$ First, Jim buys his state license, a state duck stamp, and a federal duck stamp, which comes to $68.00. All of that money goes to help wildlife.

$ Next, he needs a new pair of waders so he can slosh around in the water. This costs him $75.00. At first glance it appears that the only one benefitting from his purchase is the owner of the store, but what happens when we break it down a bit further?

Jim's purchase certainly helped the owner of the store. Because the owner's store is a success, he has many employees who rely on him for their jobs. But who else does this purchase benefit?

There's the people who
manufacture
the rubber used in
the waders.

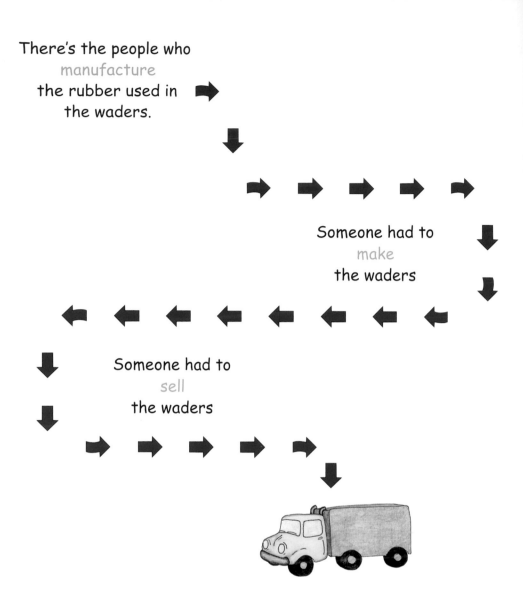

Someone had to
make
the waders

Someone had to
sell
the waders

Oh . . . we forgot the truckers who delivered the goods to the store. They had to deliver the supplies to the manufacturers as well. Did they buy fuel for their trucks? Tires? Food for themselves while they were delivering the goods? We could go on and on . . . but the point is this: Take this one purchase by this one hunter and then multiply it by 147 million! Hunters are good for the economy!

WOW!

Now You Know the Facts

Whether you choose to hunt is not important. OK, I'm lying. The future of our wildlife will depend on a new generation of hunters. The real issue of this book and the most important message I can leave you with, however, is the following truth:

Hunters play an important role in the conservation of our wildlife.

So, get off the couch. . . .
Hike, fish
Explore your natural world
Draw a duck stamp
Join a hunting group
Make a wood duck box
Get your hunter-education certificate
Become a conservationist
Hunt

It is today's hunter, not the environmentalist, who contributes the most money to sustain our wildlife. Money from hunters and hunting organizations support habitat enrichment and conservation efforts for the survival of our wildlife! Get involved today!

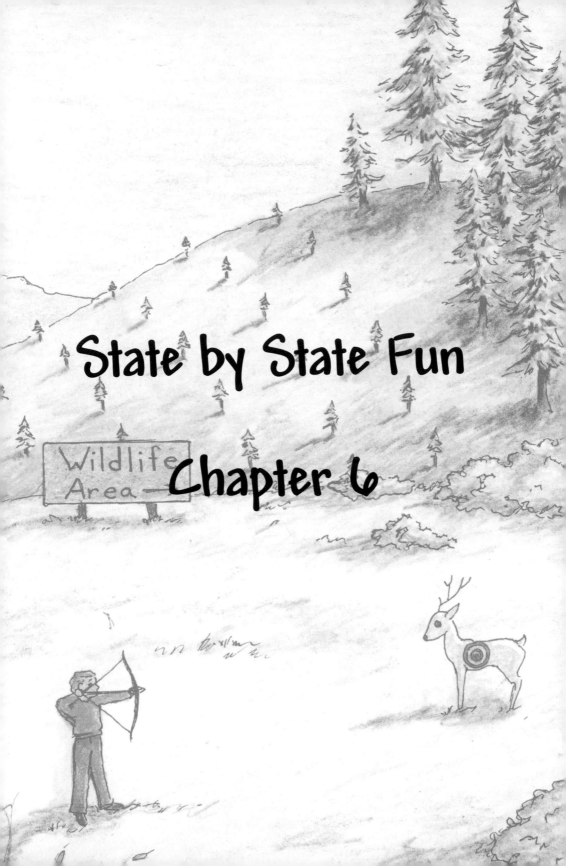

State by State Fun

Chapter 6

Wildlife
Area

Youth Programs

The programs in the box below are found in almost every state. Check them out to see what they have in your area and then go to the guide on the following pages.

Pass It On and
Outdoor Mentors Inc.
www.outdoormentors.org
1-316-290-8883

Ducks Unlimited
www.ducks.org
1-800-453-4257

Families Afield
www.familiesafield.com
1-203-426-1320

Pheasants Forever
www.pheasantsforever.com
(click on local chapters)
toll free: 1-877-773-2070

The National Rifle Association
www.nrahq.org

Scholastic Clay Target and Rifle Program

www.nssf.org/sctp

(click on State Directors on left)

Step Outside

www.stepoutside.org

1-203-426-1320

National Archery in the Schools Program (NASP)

www.nasparchery.com

(click on contacts and scroll down)

1-608-269-1779

A State by State Guide to Fun in Your Area

Use the key below to hook up with fun organizations in your area. At times, you will need to look up a local chapter on a Web site to find one. A "chapter" is a group in your area. If you don't have access to a computer, national phone numbers are listed. You may want to have an adult call to ask for a local chapter that has activities for you.

- Hunter-education courses
- 4-H Shooting Sports, state coordinators.
- The National Wild Turkey Federation, turkey hunts and activities
- Shooting programs, youth camps, and more .
- Waterfowl organizations with youth programs
- ! Don't miss these events! Fishing, hunting, archery, and more.

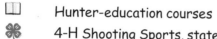 **Alabama**

- Alabama Division of Wildlife & FW Fisheries, Hunter Education, (800) 245-2740 or www.outdooralabama.com
- Emily Kling, (334) 844-2226 or e-mail: klinge@auburn.edu
- Call (800) 843-6983 or visit www.nwtf.org, then scroll down to Local Information and click on your state.
- Delta Waterfowl, go to www.deltawaterfowl.org and go to QUICK LINKS (it's on the far right-hand side), then scroll down to DELTA EVENTS until you see a map of the United States. Click your state for the local chapter. If you don't have the Internet, call (888) 987-3695.
- ! Outdoor Alabama Expo, www.outdooralabama.com, (800) 262-3151
- ! The Shooting Wire, www.shootingwire.com
- The Rocky Mountain Elk Foundation, www.rmef.com, or call (800) 225-5355

Alaska

- Alaska Department of Fish and Game, Hunter Education, (907) 267-2241 or www.wildlife.alaska.gov
- Janet Athanas, (907) 543-2248 or e-mail: janthans@cityofbethel.net
- Call (800) 843-6983 or visit www.nwtf.org, then scroll down to Local Information and click on your state.
- Youth Shooting Sports Program, (907) 267-2236 or (907) 267-2241
- Alaska NRA Youth Hunter Education Challenge, www.aimcomm.org, (907) 452-5837
- Outdoor Alaska, www.alaskaoutdoorcouncil.org, (907) 455-4262
- Delta Waterfowl, go to www.deltawaterfowl.org and go to QUICK LINKS (it's on the far right-hand side), then scroll down to DELTA EVENTS until you see a map of the United States. Click your state for the local chapter. If you don't have the Internet, call (800) 987-3695.
- The Rocky Mountain Elk Foundation, www.rmef.com, or call (800) 225-5355

Arizona

- Arizona Department of Game and Fish, Hunter Education, (623) 236-7235 or www.azgfd.gov
- Larry Neuman, (502) 297-3153 or email: neumanLM4H@aol.com
- Call (800) 843-6983 or visit www.nwtf.org, then scroll down to Local Information and click on your state.
- Arizona Deer Association, www.azdeer.org, (602) 395-DEER
- Arizona Fish and Game—youth hunting programs and shooting sports, www.azgfd.gov, (623) 236-7241
- Delta Waterfowl, go to www.deltawaterfowl.org and go to QUICK LINKS (it's on the far right-hand side), then scroll down to DELTA EVENTS until you see a map of the United States. Click your state for the local chapter. If you don't have the Internet, call (888) 987-3695.
- The Rocky Mountain Elk Foundation, www.rmef.com, or call (800) 225-5355
- Arizona Game and Fish Department Outdoor Expo (602) 942-3000

Arkansas

Arkansas Game and Fish Commission, Hunter Education,
(800)-482-5795 or www.agfc.com

Rex Roberg, (501) 671-2334 or e-mail: rroberg@uaex.edu

Call (800) 843-6983 or visit www.nwtf.org, then scroll down to Local
Information and click on your state.

Arkansas Shooting Sports Coordinator, www.agfc.com or (501) 223-6300

Delta Waterfowl, go to www.deltawaterfowl.org and go to QUICK LINKS (it's
on the far right-hand side), then scroll down to DELTA EVENTS until
you see a map of the United States. Click your state for the local
chapter. If you don't have the Internet, call (888) 987-3695.

Ducks Unlimited Greenwings Program, ar.ducks.org
(501) 728-4949

The Rocky Mountain Elk Foundation, www.rmef.com, or
call (800) 225-5355

"Youth Outdoor Expo's" Arkansas Game and Fish Commission,
(800) 482-5795

California

California Fish and Game, Hunter Education, (916) 653-9727 or
www.dfg.ca.gov/huntered/index.html

John Borba, (661) 868-6200 or e-mail: jaborba@ucdavis.edu

Call (800) 843-6983 or visit www.nwtf.org, then scroll down to Local
Information and click on your state.

Delta Waterfowl, go to www.deltawaterfowl.org and go to QUICK LINKS (it's
on the far right-hand side), then scroll down to DELTA EVENTS until
you see a map of the United States. Click your state for the local
chapter. If you don't have the Internet, call (888) 987-3695.

California Waterfowl Association, www.calwaterfowl.org,
(916) 648-1406

Cal-Deer Association, www.caldeer.org, (888) 499-3337

The Rocky Mountain Elk Foundation, www.rmef.com, or call (800) 225-5355

"Youth Outdoor Safari Day" Safari Club International, Ron Mizrahi,
(818) 952-0404 or scila@charter.net

Colorado

- Colorado Division of Wildlife, Hunter Education, (303) 291-7530 or www.wildlife.state.co.us
- (970) 491-1152 or www.colorado4h.org
- Call 1-800-843-6983 or visit www.nwtf.org, then scroll down to Local Information and click on your state.
- Delta Waterfowl, go to www.deltawaterfowl.org and go to QUICK LINKS (it's on the far right-hand side), then scroll down to DELTA EVENTS until you see a map of the United States. Click your state for the local chapter. If you don't have the Internet, call (888) 987-3695.
- The Rocky Mountain Elk Foundation, www.rmef.com, or call (800) 225-5355
- Colorado Youth Outdoors, (970) 663-0800 or info@coloradoyo.org

Connecticut

- Connecticut Conservation Education, Hunter Education, (860) 675-8130 or www.ct.gov/dep/hunting
- (860) 486-4127
- Call (800) 843-6983 or visit www.nwtf.org, then scroll down to Local Information and click on your state.
- Delta Waterfowl, go to www.deltawaterfowl.org and go to QUICK LINKS (it's on the far right-hand side), then scroll down to DELTA EVENTS until you see a map of the United States. Click your state for the local chapter. If you don't have the Internet, call (888) 987-3695.
- The Rocky Mountain Elk Foundation, www.rmef.com or call (800) 225-5355.

Delaware

- Delaware Division of Fish and Wildlife, Hunter Education, (302) 735-3600 or www.fw.delaware.gov
- (302) 831-2509
- Call (800) 843-6983 or visit www.nwtf.org, then scroll down to Local Information and click on your state.
- Delta Waterfowl, go to www.deltawaterfowl.org and go to QUICK LINKS (it's on the far right-hand side), then scroll down to DELTA EVENTS until

you see a map of the United States. Click your state for the local chapter. If you don't have the Internet, call 1-888-987-3695.

- The Rocky Mountain Elk Foundation, www.rmef.com, or call (800) 225-5355

Florida

- Florida Fish & Wildlife, Hunter Education, (850) 413-0084 or www.myfwc.com
- Albert Fuller, (352) 486-5131 or e-mail: aefu@ifas.ufl.edu
- Call (800) 843-6983 or visit www.nwtf.org, then scroll down to Local Information and click on your state.
- Delta Waterfowl, go to www.deltawaterfowl.org and go to QUICK LINKS (it's on the far right-hand side), then scroll down to DELTA EVENTS until you see a map of the United States. Click your state for the local chapter. If you don't have the Internet, call (888) 987-3695.
- The Rocky Mountain Elk Foundation, www.rmef.com, or call (800) 225-5353

Georgia

- Georgia Department of Natural Resources, Hunter Education, (770) 784-3068 or www.georgiawildlife.com
- Mark Zeigler, (678) 377-4010 or e-mail: mzeigler@uga.edu
- Call (800) 843-6983 or visit www.nwtf.org, then scroll down to Local Information and click on your state.
- Delta Waterfowl, go to www.deltawaterfowl.org and go to QUICK LINKS (it's on the far right-hand side), then scroll down to DELTA EVENTS until you see a map of the United States. Click your state for the local chapter. If you don't have the Internet, call (888) 987-3695.
- The Rocky Mountain Elk Foundation, www.rmef.com, or call (800) 225-5355
- ! Outdoor Adventure Days" Georgia Department of Natural Resources, www.georgiawildlife.com and use the search box.
- ! Georgia Outdoor Network, (800) 866-5516 or www.georgiaoutdoornetwork.com

Hawaii

- Hawaii Dept of Land and Natural Resources, Hunter Education, (808) 587-0200 or www.hawaii.gov/dlnr and go to divisions, then down to hunter education.
- Steve Nagano, (808) 453-6054 or e-mail: snagano@hawaii.edu
- Call (800) 843-6983 or visit www.nwtf.org, then scroll down to Local Information and click on your state.
- Delta Waterfowl, go to www.deltawaterfowl.org and go to QUICK LINKS (it's on the far right-hand side), then scroll down to DELTA EVENTS until you see a map of the United States. Click your state for the local chapter. If you don't have the Internet, call (888) 987-3695.

Idaho

- Idaho Fish and Game, Hunter Education, (208) 334-3746 or www.fishandgame.idaho.gov
- Arlinda Nauman, (208) 885-6321 or e-mail: anauman@uidaho.edu
- Call (800) 843-6983 or visit www.nwtf.org, then scroll down to Local Information and click on your state.
- The Rocky Mountain Elk Foundation, www.rmef.com, or call (800) 225-5355
- The Mule Deer Foundation, to find a local chapter, call toll free (888)-375-3337

Illinois

- Illinois Department of Natural Resources, Hunter Education, (217) 557-9206
- Sorry, no programs
- Call (800) 843-6983 or visit www.nwtf.org, then scroll down to Local Information and click on your state.
- Delta Waterfowl, go to www.deltawaterfowl.org and go to QUICK LINKS (it's on the far right-hand side), then scroll down to DELTA EVENTS until you see a map of the United States. Click your state for the local chapter. If you don't have the Internet, call (800) 987-3695.

❊ The Rocky Mountain Elk Foundation, www.rmef.com, or
call (800) 225-5355

"National Hunting and Fishing Days" Illinois Department of Natural
❗ Resources www.dnr.state.il.us

Indiana

⊡ Indiana Department of Natural Resources, Hunter Education,
(317) 232-4010 www.in.gov/dnr

❀ Natalie Carroll, Ph.D., (765) 494-8433 or e-mail: ncarroll@purdue.edu

🦃 Call (800) 843-6983 or visit www.nwtf.org, then scroll down to Local
Information and click on your state.

🦆 Delta Waterfowl, go to www.deltawaterfowl.org and go to QUICK LINKS (it's
on the far right-hand side), then scroll down to DELTA EVENTS until
you see a map of the United States. Click your state for the local
chapter. If you don't have the Internet, call (888) 987-3695.

❊ The Rocky Mountain Elk Foundation, www.rmef.com, or
call (800) 225-5355

"Hoosier Outdoor Expo" Indiana Department of Natural Resources,
❗ Amanda Wuestefeld, (317) 547-2075 or awustefeld@dnr.in.gov

🦆 Northwest Indiana chapter of Waterfowl USA, (219) 322-1545 or go to
www.nwiwusa.com and click on youth programs on the left.

Iowa

⊡ Iowa Department of Natural Resources, Hunter Education,
(515) 281-5918 or www.iowadnr.com

❀ Bryan Whaley, (515) 332-2201 or e-mail: bwhaley@iastate.edu

🦃 Call (800) 843-6983 or visit www.nwtf.org, then scroll down to Local
Information and click on your state.

🦆 Delta Waterfowl, go to www.deltawaterfowl.org and go to QUICK LINKS (it's
on the far right-hand side), then scroll down to DELTA EVENTS until
you see a map of the United States. Click your state for the local
chapter. If you don't have the Internet, call (888) 987-3695.

❊ The Rocky Mountain Elk Foundation, www.rmef.com, or
call (800) 225-5355

Kansas

- Kansas Department of Wildlife and Parks, Hunter Education, (620) 672-5911 or www.kdwp.state.ks.us
- Gary Gerhard, (785) 532-5800 or e-mail: ggerhard@oznet.ksu.edu
- Call (800) 843-6983 or visit www.nwtf.org, then scroll down to Local Information and click on your state.
- Delta Waterfowl, go to www.deltawaterfowl.org and go to QUICK LINKS (it's on the far right-hand side), then scroll down to DELTA EVENTS until you see a map of the United States. Click your state for the local chapter. If you don't have the Internet, call (888) 987-3695.
- The Rocky Mountain Elk Foundation, www.rmef.com, or call (800) 225-5355

Kentucky

- Kentucky Dept. of Fish and Wildlife Resources, Hunter Education, (800) 852-0942 or www.fw.ky.gov
- Marion Creech, (502) 252-8811 or e-mail: jcreech@uky.edu
- Call (800) 843-6983 or visit www.nwtf.org, then scroll down to Local Information and click on your state.
- Delta Waterfowl, go to www.deltawaterfowl.org and go to QUICK LINKS (it's on the far right-hand side), then scroll down to DELTA EVENTS until you see a map of the United States. Click your state for the local chapter. If you don't have the Internet, call (888) 987-3695.
- The Rocky Mountain Elk Foundation, www.rmef.com, or call (800) 225-5355

Louisiana

- Louisiana Department of Wildlife Fisheries, Hunter Education, (225) 765-2932 or www.wlf.state.la.us
- David Boldt, (225) 578-6644 or e-mail: dboldt@agcenter.lsu.edu
- Call (800) 843-6983 or visit www.nwtf.org, then scroll down to Local Information and click on your state.
- Delta Waterfowl, go to www.deltawaterfowl.org and go to QUICK LINKS

(it's on the far right-hand side), then scroll down to DELTA EVENTS until you see a map of the United States. Click your state for the local chapter. If you don't have the Internet, call (888) 987-3695.

The Rocky Mountain Elk Foundation, www.rmef.com or
     call (800) 225-5355

! "Louisiana Wildlife and Fisheries Outdoor Expo" Louisiana Department of Wildlife and Fisheries, (225) 765-2932
     or www.wlf.louisiana.gov

Maine

Maine Dept. of Inland Fisheries and Wildlife, Hunter Education,
     (207) 287-5220, or www.state.me.us/ifw

Dr. Fred Schlutt, (207) 581-1162 or e-mail: fschlutt@umext.maine.edu

Call (800) 843-6983 or visit www.nwtf.org, then scroll down to Local
     Information and click on your state.

Delta Waterfowl, go to www.deltawaterfowl.org and go to QUICK LINKS (it's on the far right-hand side), then scroll down to DELTA EVENTS until you see a map of the United States. Click your state for the local chapter. If you don't have the Internet, call (888) 987-3695.

The Rocky Mountain Elk Foundation, www.rmef.com or
     call (800) 225-5355

! Maine Youth Fish and Game, www.maineyouthfishandgame.org

Maryland

Maryland Natural Resources Police, Hunter Education,
     (410) 643-8502 or www.dnr.state.md.us

Conrad Arnold, (410) 228-8800, e-mail: carnold@umd.edu

Call (800) 843-6983 or visit www.nwtf.org, then scroll down to Local
     Information and click on your state.

Delta Waterfowl, go to www.deltawaterfowl.org and go to QUICK LINKS (it's on the far right-hand side), then scroll down to DELTA EVENTS until you see a map of the United States. Click your state for the local chapter. If you don't have the Internet, call (888) 987-3695.

The Rocky Mountain Elk Foundation, www.rmef.com, or call (800) 225-5355

! Maryland National Fishing and Hunting Day,
www.dnr.state.md.us/wildlife/NHFD/index.asp
or Patricia Allen (410) 260-8537

Massachusetts

☐ Massachusetts Division of Fisheries and Wildlife, Hunter Education,
(978) 632-7648 or www.state.ma.us/dfwele

❀ Sorry, no programs!

🦃 Call (800) 843-6983 or visit www.nwtf.org, then scroll down to Local
Information and click on your state.

🦆 Delta Waterfowl, go to www.deltawaterfowl.org and go to QUICK LINKS (it's
on the far right-hand side), then scroll down to DELTA EVENTS until
you see a map of the United States. Click your state for the local
chapter. If you don't have the Internet, call (888) 987-3695.

🦌 The Rocky Mountain Elk Foundation, www.rmef.com, or
call (800) 225-5355

! "Massachusetts Outdoor Expo" Mass. Department of Fish and Wildlife
Gary Sima, (508) 389-6314 or www.fawnsociety.com

! Junior Hunters.Org, all types of hunting programs. www.juniorhunters.org
or (508) 393-5333

Michigan

☐ Michigan Dept. of Natural Resources, Hunter Education,
(517) 335-3418 or www.michigandnr.com

❀ Dale Elshoff, (517) 432-7651 or e-mail: elshoff@msu.edu

🦃 Call (800) 843-6983 or visit www.nwtf.org, then scroll down to Local
Information and click on your state.

🦆 Delta Waterfowl, go to www.deltawaterfowl.org and go to QUICK LINKS
(it's on the far right-hand side), then scroll down to DELTA
EVENTS until you see a map of the United States. Click your
state for the local chapter. If you don't have the Internet, call
(888) 987-3695.

🦌 The Rocky Mountain Elk Foundation, www.rmef.com, or call (800) 225-5355

🦆 Michigan Duck Hunters Association, www.midha.org or call (906) 842-3423

Minnesota

- Minnesota Dept. of Natural Resources, Hunter Education,
  (800) 366-8917 or www.dnr.state.mn.us
- Kia Harries, (507) 372-3908 or e-mail: kharries@umn.edu
- Call (800) 843-6983 or visit www.nwtf.org, then scroll down to Local
  Information and click on your state.
- Delta Waterfowl, go to www.deltawaterfowl.org and go to QUICK LINKS (it's
  on the far right-hand side), then scroll down to DELTA EVENTS until
  you see a map of the United States. Click your state for the local
  chapter. If you don't have the Internet, call (888) 987-3695.
- The Rocky Mountain Elk Foundation, www.rmef.com, or
  call (800) 225-5355
- Minnesota Waterfowl Association, www.mnwaterfowl.com.
  Check out Woodie Camp on the left, or call (952) 767-0320

Mississippi

- Mississippi Dept. of Wildlife, Hunter Education, (601) 432-2182 or
  www.mdc.mo.gov
- Dr. Susan Holder, (662) 325-3352 or e-mail: susanh@ext.msstate.edu
- Call (800) 843-6983 or visit www.nwtf.org, then scroll down to Local
  Information and click on your state.
- Delta Waterfowl, go to www.deltawaterfowl.org and go to QUICK LINKS (it's
  on the far right-hand side), then scroll down to DELTA EVENTS until
  you see a map of the United States. Click your state for the local
  chapter. If you don't have the Internet, call (888) 987-3695.
- The Rocky Mountain Elk Foundation, www.rmef.com, or call (800) 225-5355
- Mississippi Valley Duck Hunters Association, www.mvdha.com, check out
  their Young Ducks program

Missouri

- Missouri Department of Conservation, Hunter Education,
  (573) 751-4115 or www.mdc.mo.gov
- Gerry Snapp, (573) 882-5547 or e-mail: snappg@missouri.edu

- Call (800) 843-6983 or visit www.nwtf.org, then scroll down to Local Information and click on your state.
- Delta Waterfowl, go to www.deltawaterfowl.org and go to QUICK LINKS (it's on the far right-hand side), then scroll down to DELTA EVENTS until you see a map of the United States. Click your state for the local chapter. If you don't have the Internet, call (888) 987-3695.
- The Rocky Mountain Elk Foundation, www.rmef.com, or call (800) 225-5355
- Missouri Waterfowl Association, www.mowaterfowl.org

Montana

- Montana Fish, Wildlife and Parks, Hunter Education, (406) 444-3188 or www.fwp.state.mt.us
- Todd Kesner, (406) 944-3501 or e-mail: tkesner@montana.edu
- Call (800) 843-6983 or visit www.nwtf.org, then scroll down to Local Information and click on your state.
- The Rocky Mountain Elk Foundation, www.rmef.com, or call (800) 225-5355

Nebraska

- Nebraska Game and Parks Commission, Hunter Education, (402) 471-0641 or www.ngpc.state.ne.us
- Steve Pritchard, (402) 395-2158 or e-mail: spritchard1@unl.edu
- Call (800) 843-6983 or visit www.nwtf.org, then scroll down to Local Information and click on your state.
- Delta Waterfowl, go to www.deltawaterfowl.org and go to QUICK LINKS (it's on the far right-hand side), then scroll down to DELTA EVENTS until you see a map of the United States. Click your state for the local chapter. If you don't have the Internet, call (888) 987-3695.
- The Rocky Mountain Elk Foundation, www.rmef.com or call (800) 225-5355
- "Nebraska Outdoor Expo and Missouri River Outdoor Expo" (402) 471-6009 or www.nebraskaoutdoorsexpo.org

Nevada

- Nevada Department of Wildlife, Hunter Education,
    (775) 688-1500 or www.ndow.org
- Stephen R. Schafer, (775) 784-6207 or e-mail: schafers@unce.unr.edu
- Call (800) 843-6983 or visit www.nwtf.org, then scroll down to Local
    Information and click on your state.
- The Rocky Mountain Elk Foundation, www.rmef.com, or
    call (800) 225-5355
- Nevada Waterfowl Association, www.nevadawaterfowl.org or
    (775) 853-8331

New Hampshire

- New Hampshire Fish and Game Dept., Hunter Education,
    (603) 271-3212 or www.wildlife.state.nh.us
- Larry Barker, (603) 788-4961 or e-mail: larry.barker@unh.edu
- Call (800) 843-6983 or visit www.nwtf.org, then scroll down to Local
    Information and click on your state.
- Delta Waterfowl, go to www.deltawaterfowl.org and go to QUICK LINKS
    (it's on the far right-hand side), then scroll down to DELTA EVENTS
    until you see a map of the United States. Click your state for the
    local chapter. If you don't have the Internet,
    call (888) 987-3695.
- The Rocky Mountain Elk Foundation, www.rmef.com or
    call (800) 225-5355

New Jersey

- New Jersey Division of Fish and Wildlife, Hunter Education,
    (908) 735-7040 or (877) 2HUNTING or www.njfishandwildlife.com
- James A. Tavares, (973) 948-3550 or e-mail: Tavares@aesop.rutgers.edu
- Call (800) 843-6983 or visit www.nwtf.org, then scroll down to Local
    Information and click on your state.
- Delta Waterfowl, go to www.deltawaterfowl.org and go to QUICK LINKS
    (it's on the far right-hand side), then scroll down to DELTA EVENTS

until you see a map of the United States. Click your state for the local chapter. If you don't have the Internet, call (888) 987-3695.

🦌 The Rocky Mountain Elk Foundation, www.rmef.com or
    call (800) 225-5355

🔫 New Mexico

📖 New Mexico Game and Fish, Hunter Education, (505) 222-4731 or
    www.wildlife.state.nm.us
🍀 Rick Richardson, (505) 646-1157 or e-mail: frrichar@nmsu.edu
🦃 Call (800) 843-6983 or visit www.nwtf.org, then scroll down to Local
    Information and click on your state.
🦆 Delta Waterfowl, go to www.deltawaterfowl.org and go to QUICK LINKS (it's
    on the far right-hand side), then scroll down to DELTA EVENTS until
    you see a map of the United States. Click your state for the local
    chapter. If you don't have the Internet, call (888) 987-3695.
🦌 The Rocky Mountain Elk Foundation, www.rmef.com or
    call (800) 225-5355
❗ "New Mexico Outdoor Expo" New Mexico Department of Game and Fish,
    (505) 222-4731

🔫 New York

📖 New York Dept. of Env. Conservation, Hunter Education, (888) 486-8332
    Michael Mathews, mjmatthe@gw.dec.state.ny.us
🍀 Kenyon Simpson, (518) 885-8995 or e-mail: krs36@cornell.edu
🦃 Call (800) 843-6983 or visit www.nwtf.org, then scroll down to Local
    Information and click on your state.
🦆 Delta Waterfowl, go to www.deltawaterfowl.org and go to QUICK LINKS
    (it's on the far right-hand side), then scroll down to DELTA EVENTS
    until you see a map of the United States. Click your state for the
    local chapter. If you don't have the Internet,
    call (888) 987-3695.
🦌 The Rocky Mountain Elk Foundation, www.rmef.com or
    call (800) 225-5355

North Carolina

- North Carolina Wildlife Resources Commission, Hunter Education, (919) 707-0031 or www.ncwildlife.org
- Gene Shutt, (910) 652-5905 or e-mail: rshutt@etInternet.net
- Call (800) 843-6983 or visit www.nwtf.org, then scroll down to Local Information and click on your state.
- Delta Waterfowl, go to www.deltawaterfowl.org and go to QUICK LINKS (it's on the far right-hand side), then scroll down to DELTA EVENTS until you see a map of the United States. Click your state for the local chapter. If you don't have the Internet, call (888) 987-3695.
- The Rocky Mountain Elk Foundation, www.rmef.com, or call (800) 225-5355.

North Dakota

- North Dakota Game and Fish Department, Hunter Education, (701) 328-6615, John Hanson, jdhanson@nd.gov
- Adrian Biewer, Adrian.biewer@ndsu.edu (701) 231-6184
- Call (800) 843-6983 or visit www.nwtf.org, then scroll down to Local Information and click on your state.
- Delta Waterfowl, go to www.deltawaterfowl.org and go to QUICK LINKS (it's on the far right-hand side), then scroll down to DELTA EVENTS until you see a map of the United States. Click your state for the local chapter. If you don't have the Internet, call (888) 987-3695.
- The Rocky Mountain Elk Foundation, www.rmef.com, or call (800) 225-5355

Ohio

- Ohio Division of Wildlife, Hunter Education, (800) WILDLIFE or www.ohiodnr.com
- Larry Harris, (740) 286-4058 or harris.870@osu.edu
- Call (800) 843-6983 or visit www.nwtf.org, then scroll down to Local Information and click on your state.
- Delta Waterfowl, go to www.deltawaterfowl.org and go to QUICK LINKS (it's on the far right-hand side), then scroll down to DELTA EVENTS

until you see a map of the United States. Click your state for the local chapter. If you don't have the Internet, call (888) 987-3695.

- The Rocky Mountain Elk Foundation, www.rmef.com or call (800) 225-5355

Oklahoma

- Oklahoma Division of Wildlife Conservation, Hunter Education, (405) 522-4572 or www.wildlifedepartment.com
- Charles Cox, (405) 744-8885 or e-mail: ccox@okstate.edu
- Call (800) 843-6983 or visit www.nwtf.org, then scroll down to Local Information and click on your state.
- Delta Waterfowl, go to www.deltawaterfowl.org and go to QUICK LINKS (it's on the far right-hand side), then scroll down to DELTA EVENTS until you see a map of the United States. Click your state for the local chapter. If you don't have the Internet, call (888) 987-3695.
- The Rocky Mountain Elk Foundation, www.rmef.com, or call (800) 225-5355
- ! "Oklahoma Wildlife Expo" Oklahoma Department of Wildlife Conservation, Rhonda Hurst, (405) 522-6279 or rhurst@odwc.state.ok.us

Oregon

- Oregon Department of Fish and Wildlife, Hunter Education, (503) 947-6016 or www.dfw.state.or.gov
- 4-H Youth Development (541) 737-2421
- Call (800) 843-6983 or visit www.nwtf.org, then scroll down to Local Information and click on your state.
- Delta Waterfowl, go to www.deltawaterfowl.org and go to QUICK LINKS (it's on the far right-hand side), then scroll down to DELTA EVENTS until you see a map of the United States. Click your state for the local chapter. If you don't have the Internet, call (888) 987-3695.

- The Rocky Mountain Elk Foundation, www.rmef.com or
     call (800) 225-5355
- Ducks Unlimited Oregon Outdoor Youth Day, contact Ducks Unlimited at
     www.ducks.org and search Oregon for events

Pennsylvania

- Pennsylvania Game Commission, Hunter Education, (717) 787-4250
     or www.pgc.state.pa.us
- Joe Fuller, (570) 278-1158 or e-mail: SusquehannaExt@psu.edu
- Call (800) 843-6983 or visit www.nwtf.org, then scroll down to Local
     Information and click on your state.
- Delta Waterfowl, go to www.deltawaterfowl.org and go to QUICK LINKS
     (it's on the far right-hand side), then scroll down to DELTA EVENTS
     until you see a map of the United States. Click your state for the
     local chapter. If you don't have the Internet,
     call (888) 987-3695.
- The Rocky Mountain Elk Foundation, www.rmef.com, or
     call (800) 225-5355
- Pymatuning Lake Outdoor Expo, www.pymatuninglake.com or call
     Lee Walker (814) 382-8551 with Ducks Unlimited

Rhode Island

- Rhode Island Department of Fish and Game, Hunter Education,
     (401) 789-3094 or www.dem.ri.gov
- Christy Horan (401) 874-2959
- Call (800) 843-6983 or visit www.nwtf.org, then scroll down to Local
     Information and click on your state.
- Delta Waterfowl, go to www.deltawaterfowl.org and go to QUICK LINKS
     (it's on the far right-hand side), then scroll down to DELTA EVENTS
     until you see a map of the United States. Click your state for the
     local chapter. If you don't have the Internet,
     call (888) 987-3695.
- Rocky Mountain Elk Foundation, www.rmef.com or
     call (800) 225-5355

South Carolina

📖 South Carolina Department of Natural Resources, Hunter Education,
(800) 277-4301 or www.dnr.sc.gov

🍀 Rick Willey, (864) 656-3090 or e-mail: rwlly@clemson.edu

🦃 Call (800) 843-6983 or visit www.nwtf.org, then scroll down to Local
Information and click on your state.

🦆 Delta Waterfowl, go to www.deltawaterfowl.org and go to QUICK LINKS (it's
on the far right-hand side), then scroll down to DELTA EVENTS until
you see a map of the United States. Click your state for the local
chapter. If you don't have the Internet, call (888) 987-3695.

🦌 The Rocky Mountain Elk Foundation, www.rmef.com, or call (800) 225-5355

❗ "National Fishing and Hunting Day—An Adventure in the Outdoors"
(803) 256-0670 South Carolina Wildlife Federation

🦆 South Carolina Waterfowl Association, check out Camp Woodie,
(803) 452-6001 or www.scwa.org

South Dakota

📖 South Dakota Dept. of Game, Fish and Parks, Hunter Education,
(605) 773-3485 or www.sdgfp.info

🍀 Kathy Reeves, (605) 394-2236 or e-mail: reeves.kathryn@ces.sdstate.edu

🦃 Call (800) 843-6983 or visit www.nwtf.org, then scroll down to Local
Information and click on your state.

🦆 Delta Waterfowl, go to www.deltawaterfowl.org and go to QUICK LINKS (it's
on the far right-hand side), then scroll down to DELTA EVENTS until
you see a map of the United States. Click your state for the local
chapter. If you don't have the Internet, call (888) 987-3695.

🦌 The Rocky Mountain Elk Foundation, www.rmef.com or call (800) 225-5355

❗ "South Dakota Outdoor Expo—Explore the Outdoors"
(605) 353-7340 or www.sdoutdoorexpo.com

Tennessee

📖 Tennessee Wildlife Resources Agency, Hunter Education, (615) 781-6538 or
www.state.tn.us

❀ Daniel Sarver, (865) 974-2128 or e-mail: dsarver@tennessee.edu

🦃 Call (800) 843-6983 or visit www.nwtf.org, then scroll down to Local
　　　Information and click on your state.

🦆 Delta Waterfowl, go to www.deltawaterfowl.org and go to QUICK LINKS
　　　(it's on the far right-hand side), then scroll down to DELTA EVENTS
　　　until you see a map of the United States. Click your state for the
　　　local chapter. If you don't have the Internet,
　　　call (888) 987-3695.

🦌 The Rocky Mountain Elk Foundation, www.rmef.com, or call (800) 225-5355

🔫 Texas

📖 Texas Parks and Wildlife Department, Hunter Education,
　　　(800) 792-1112 or www.tpwd.state.tx.us

❀ Ron Howard, (979) 845-1214 or e-mail: ra-howard@tamu.edu

🦃 Call (800) 843-6983 or visit www.nwtf.org, then scroll down to Local
　　　Information and click on your state.

🦆 Delta Waterfowl, go to www.deltawaterfowl.org and go to QUICK LINKS
　　　(it's on the far right-hand side), then scroll down to DELTA EVENTS
　　　until you see a map of the United States. Click your state for the
　　　local chapter. If you don't have the Internet,
　　　call (888) 987-3695.

🦌 The Rocky Mountain Elk Foundation, www.rmef.com, or
　　　call (800) 225-5355

❗ "Texas Parks and Wildlife Expo" Texas Parks and Wildlife Department,
　　　trey.hamlet@tpwd.state.tx.us , (512) 389-4361

🔫 Utah

📖 Utah Division of Wildlife, Hunter Education, (801) 538-4726 or
　　　www.wildlife.utah.gov

❀ Richard Beard, (435) 797-0573 or e-mail: rbeard@cc.usu.edu

🦃 Call (800) 843-6983 or visit www.nwtf.org, then scroll down to Local
　　　Information and click on your state.

🦆 Delta Waterfowl, go to www.deltawaterfowl.org and go to QUICK LINKS
　　　(it's on the far right-hand side), then scroll down to DELTA EVENTS

until you see a map of the United States. Click your state for the local chapter. If you don't have the Internet, call (888) 987-3695.

🦌 The Rocky Mountain Elk Foundation, www.rmef.com or call (800) 225-5355

Vermont

📖 Vermont Department of Fish and Game, Hunter Education, (802) 241-3720 or www.vtfishandwildlife.com

🍀 Lisa J. Muzzey, (802) 885-8386 or e-mail: lisa.muzzey@uvm.edu

🦃 Call (800) 843-6983 or visit www.nwtf.org, then scroll down to Local Information and click on your state.

🦆 Delta Waterfowl, go to www.deltawaterfowl.org and go to QUICK LINKS (it's on the far right-hand side), then scroll down to DELTA EVENTS until you see a map of the United States. Click your state for the local chapter. If you don't have the Internet, call (888) 987-3695.

🦌 The Rocky Mountain Elk Foundation, www.rmef.com or call (800) 225-5355

Virginia

📖 Virginia Dept. of Game and Inland Fisheries, Hunter Education, (540) 899-4169 or www.dgif.virginia.gov

🍀 Jinx Baney, (434) 848-2151 or e-mail: jbaney@vt.edu

🦃 Call (800) 843-6983 or visit www.nwtf.org, then scroll down to Local Information and click on your state.

🦆 Delta Waterfowl, go to www.deltawaterfowl.org and go to QUICK LINKS (it's on the far right-hand side), then scroll down to DELTA EVENTS until you see a map of the United States. Click your state for the local chapter. If you don't have the Internet, call (800) 987-3695.

🦌 The Rocky Mountain Elk Foundation, www.rmef.com or call (800) 225-5355

❗ Virginia Waterfowl Association, www.vawfa.org

Washington

- Washington Dept. of Fish and Wildlife, Hunter Education,
  (360) 902-8112 or www.wdfw.wa.gov
- Janet Schmidt, (509) 397-6290, e-mail: Schmidt@wsu.edu
- Call (800) 843-6983 or visit www.nwtf.org, then scroll down to Local
  Information and click on your state.
- Delta Waterfowl, go to www.deltawaterfowl.org and go to QUICK LINKS (it's
  on the far right-hand side), then scroll down to DELTA EVENTS until
  you see a map of the United States. Click your state for the local
  chapter. If you don't have the Internet, call (888) 987-3695.
- The Rocky Mountain Elk Foundation, www.rmef.com, or call (800) 225-5355
- ! "Washington Youth Outdoor Adventure Expo" Go Play Outside Alliance and
  Washington Department of Fish and Wildlife. Keith Underwood,
  (360) 902-8112

West Virginia

- West Virginia Div. of Natural Resources, Hunter Education,
  (304) 558-2784 or www.wvdnr.gov
- Jean Woloshuk, (304) 293-6131 or e-mail: jwoloshu@wvu.edu
- Call (800) 843-6983 or visit www.nwtf.org, then scroll down to Local
  Information and click on your state.
- Delta Waterfowl, go to www.deltawaterfowl.org and go to QUICK LINKS (it's
  on the far right-hand side), then scroll down to DELTA EVENTS until
  you see a map of the United States. Click your state for the local
  chapter. If you don't have the Internet, call (888) 987-3695.
- The Rocky Mountain Elk Foundation, www.rmef.com or call (800) 225-5355
- ! "West Virginia Celebration of National Hunting and Fishing Days,"
  W.V. Department of Natural Resources, Jerry Westfall,
  (304) 558-2771 or jerrywestfall@wvdnr.gov

Wisconsin

- Wisconsin Dept. of Natural Resources, Hunter Education,
  (608) 266-2143 or www.dnr.state.wi.us

- Steve Kinzel, (608) 262-1536 or e-mail: steve.kinzel@uwex.edu
- Call (800) 843-6983 or visit www.nwtf.org, then scroll down to Local Information and click on your state.
- Delta Waterfowl, go to www.deltawaterfowl.org and go to QUICK LINKS (it's on the far right-hand side), then scroll down to DELTA EVENTS until you see a map of the United States. Click your state for the local chapter. If you don't have the Internet, call (888) 987-3695.
- The Rocky Mountain Elk Foundation, www.rmef.com or call (800) 225-5355
- "Wisconsin Outdoor Education Expo" Wisconsin Outdoor Alliance, Heidi Hubble, (608) 833-2040 or heidihubble@tds.net
- Wisconsin Waterfowl Association, www.widucks.org. Check out their Outdoor Adventure Days or call (800) 524-8460

Wyoming

- Wyoming Game and Fish Dept., Hunter Education, (307) 777-4538 or gf.state.wy.us
- Warren Crawford, (307) 766-5170 or e-mail: Crawford@uwyo.edu
- Call (800) 843-6983 or visit www.nwtf.org, then scroll down to Local Information and click on your state.
- Delta Waterfowl, go to www.deltawaterfowl.org and go to QUICK LINKS (it's on the far right-hand side), then scroll down to DELTA EVENTS until you see a map of the United States. Click your state for the local chapter. If you don't have the Internet, call (888) 987-3695.
- The Rocky Mountain Elk Foundation, www.rmef.com or call (800) 225-5355
- "Wyoming Hunting and Fishing Heritage Expo" Wyoming Game and Fish Department, (888) EXP-OWYO or gf.state.wy.us and click on link

Recycle

Go Green

DON'T EAT MEAT

Save the planet

Save the polar bears

**With so many messages out there,
what's a kid to do?**

Hike
Fish
Go to camp
Plant a tree
Draw a Duck Stamp
Join a hunting group
Build a wood duck box
Send your teacher to school
Explore your natural world

Get your hunter-education certificate

Hunt